*S*oliloquies

The Augustine Series

Selected writings from "The Works of Saint Augustine—
A Translation for the 21st Century"

Volume II

Soliloquies
Augustine's Interior Dialogue

Saint Augustine

*S*oliloquies

Augustine's Interior Dialogue

Translation and Notes by
Kim Paffenroth

Introduction by
Boniface Ramsey, O.P.

Edited by
John E. Rotelle, O.S.A.

New City Press
www.newcitypress.com

Published in the United States by New City Press
202 Cardinal Rd., Hyde Park, NY 12538
www.newcitypress.com
©2000 Augustine Heritage Institute, Inc . All rights reserved.

Cover design by Nick Cianfarani

Library of Congress Cataloging-in-Publication Data:
  Augustine, Saint, Bishop of Hippo.
      [Selections. English. 1999]
      The Augustine series / Saint Augustine.
          p.   cm.
      Includes bibliographical references.
      ISBN 1-56548-124-0 (pbk.: v. 1)
      1. Theology--Early works to 1800.   I. Title.
  BR65.A73E5   1999
  230'.14--dc21   99-18777
                                                                CIP

Nihil Obstat: John E. Rotelle, O.S.A., S.T.L., Censor Deputatus
Imprimatur: +Patrick Sheridan, DD, Vicar General, Archdiocese of New York
            Archdiocese of New York, July 22, 1999

Printed in Canada

Contents

Soliloquies

Book I

Book II

Introduction

The two books of the *Soliloquies* were written at Cassiciacum, near Lake Como in northern Italy. There Augustine had retired with his mother Monica, his son Adeodatus, his brother Navigius, and a few friends, and there he stayed in their company from early autumn of 386 until perhaps January or February of 387. It was a significant period in Augustine's life, a classic time of transition: he had left Milan following the dramatic conversion recorded in a famous passage at the end of the eighth book of the *Confessions* and was now enjoying a purposeful leisure in anticipation of his baptism, which would occur at Easter of 387, back in Milan.

These four or five months of rural retreat, passed in the midst of a small community of like-minded persons far from the clamor of Milan, saw the production of a number of works — *Answer to the Academics*, *The Happy Life*, and *Order*, in addition to the *Soliloquies* themselves. Common to all of these writings — the first of Augustine's to have survived — is what we might characterize as their philosophical preoccupation, as well as the dialogical form that was in vogue in antiquity.

The philosophical thrust of these works has exercised commentators for decades. Why, so soon after his decisive conversion, it is asked, would their author have shown so much interest in philosophical questions and so little with regard to specifically Christian issues? For there is, in fact, very little direct mention of Christ in any of these treatises (the name of Christ does not appear in the *Soliloquies*, although "the one who is begotten," the Second Person of the Trinity, is referred to in passing in I, 1, 4), nor does the God who is spoken of in them seem all too far removed from the God of the philosophers (one need only consult the lengthy prayer that Augustine utters toward the very beginning of the *Soliloquies*, in I, 1, 2-6), nor are the problems addressed in them — the nature of truth, for example, or the immortality of the soul — such as might not have been gladly addressed by pagan philosophers.

These works may be disappointingly low in Christian content for one so recently converted, but on the other hand they are certainly not un-Christian or anti-Christian. They suggest that Augustine wanted only a solidly scriptural faith (Ambrose had already begun to unlock the deeper meaning of the scriptures to him perhaps as little as a year previously, as we may read in *Confessions* VI, 4, 6) but also one that was philosophically defensible, so far as that might be possible. Perhaps no Father of the Church lays so much stress on the inexplicability of the divine plan as does Augustine, particularly in his later years when he is battling Pelagianism, and Augustine's treatises, while not necessarily anti-intellectual, are nonetheless filled with cautions about the risks incurred by the overreaching intellect and about the limitations of philosophy. Still, no Father is as intellectually probing as he, nor as methodical and systematic in his probing, with the possible exceptions of Origen and Gregory of Nyssa. He may have had reservations about the workings of the mind, but he would take the mind as far as it would go. It is not surprising, then, if the *Soliloquies* and the other early treatises in question demonstrate this tendency.

Moreover, Augustine simply did not at this point have the Christian background necessary for writing a more resonantly Christian work, and he would not begin to acquire this background until he had returned home to North Africa in 388 and spent some years meditating on scripture.

The yearning of a gifted (but also somewhat untested) mind for higher things, for truth and for God, and also a certain lack of Christian amplitude, are qualities, therefore, that inevitably strike the reader of the *Soliloquies*. But because the author of the *Soliloquies* was also to be the author of the *Confessions, The City of God, The Trinity,* and numerous other writings that have indelibly marked not only Western Christianity but also Western civilization, and because the path from the *Soliloquies* to these later and grander works is not so very indirect, it is well worth reading the earlier work.

Augustine's earliest surviving writings are, as has been noted, in dialogue form. But what makes the *Soliloquies* radically different from the others is that their dialogue is a wholly interior one, between Augustine and his own reason, whereas the others involve Augustine and his fellow "retreatants" at Cassiciacum. "I question myself and I respond to myself," Augustine explains in *Revisions* I, 4, 1, when he reviews the *Soliloquies*, "as if reason and I were two, although I was alone." This approach had no precedent in Christian literature. Indeed, the very title of the work, which expresses this inner interchange, is, from all we can tell, a word coined by Augustine (II, 7, 14) — *soliloquia*, a "speaking alone," or "conversations alone."

The special form of the *Soliloquies*, with its pattern of intense interiority, looks forward to all those other writings of Augustine that are characterized by the same quality — most notably, of course, the *Confessions*. This style, far more than that of the customary dialogue between two persons, suggests a kind of tentativeness, uncertainty, sense of quest, which is all the clearer in that the "Augustine" of the dialogue is a seeker, whereas "reason" responds confidently to the questions that Augustine poses and provokes him to ask still others. In fact, throughout his writings Augustine is far more tentative and unapodictic than he is usually given credit for, and the shape of the *Soliloquies* hints at that lifetime trait.

The quest that the *Soliloquies* make is for "God and the soul," the only two things worth knowing, as Augustine declares in an oft-quoted phrase (I, 2, 7). But the search stops slightly short of its goal. Augustine himself explains what he has accomplished, and left unaccomplished, in *Revisions* I, 4, 1:

> In the first book there is a search for and to a certain extent a discovery of what kind of person one must be if one wants to acquire wisdom, which is by no means acquired by the bodily senses but by the mind, and at the end of the book it is concluded, after a certain process of reasoning, that those things which truly are, are immortal. In the second book the matter of the soul's immortality is treated at length but incompletely.

The very end of the treatise makes mention of another work that will round out the *Soliloquies* (II, 20, 36). We know from *Revisions* (I, 5, 1) that this other work is the book on *The Immortality of the Soul*, which was written quite soon after the *Soliloquies*, when Augustine had left Cassiciacum and returned to Milan.

When we analyze the *Soliloquies*, as we shall now do in a cursory fashion, we notice that the theme of search — "for myself and my own good, and for what evil should be avoided" — is announced at the very outset of the work (I, 1, 1). The long prayer that occupies all but a small part of the first chapter serves both as an act of supplication, so that the search may be successful, and as something of a description of the God who must be searched for (I, 1, 2-6). The scope of the search is then made precise in the words already alluded to: "*Augustine:* I want to know God and the soul. *Reason:* Nothing more? *Augustine:* Nothing whatsoever" (I, 2, 7).

How to obtain a sufficient knowledge of God? First, the senses are to be rejected as means of this knowledge (I, 3, 8). The study of geometry is unsatisfactory as an analogue to the degree that, although it does not make use of sense knowledge, its object is utterly different than God (I, 5, 11). Faith, hope, and love, it is concluded, alone can bring the soul to the vision or knowledge of God; it is these that make the soul healthy and render it capable of seeing.

But certain things can obscure the sight even of spiritually healthy eyes. In a lengthy passage Augustine sets out some of these hindrances — wealth, honor, the love of a wife, the pleasures of the palate, friends, life itself, and, finally, bodily pain. Each of them, however, is dismissed, for Augustine professes to be so much in love with wisdom, the knowledge of God, that they cannot stand in his way (I, 10, 17 — 13, 23). With that the *Soliloquies* are interrupted so that Augustine can get a night's rest.

The following day's dialogue, which takes up the brief remainder of the first book, is a preparation for the discussion on the nature of the soul. The substance of it, succinctly put, is that, inasmuch as the truth is immortal, it can only exist in immortal things (I, 15, 29). This sets the stage for the second book, which follows what appears to be another interlude of indeterminate duration.

The second book commences on an affective note that is typically Augustinian — that of yearning: "Our work has been interrupted long enough; love is impatient, and there will be no end to tears, unless love is given what it loves. Therefore let us begin the second book" (II, 1, 1). With that Augustine says a prayer of exceeding brevity that reprises the famous words of the *Soliloquies* (I, 2, 7): "God, who is always the same, may I know myself, may I know you" (II, 1, 1).

The dialogue proceeds with Augustine's avowal that what he wants to know first about himself is whether or not he is immortal. Immortality, however, is worthless without knowledge, and knowledge in turn brings with it happiness. Immortality, therefore, is the necessary preliminary to knowledge and happiness, the recognition of which fact lies at the bottom of Augustine's desire to assure himself that he possesses this quality.

The rest of the discussion, then, beginning with a resumption of the interchange on the immortality of truth that concluded the first book (II, 2, 2), is occupied with demonstrating that the soul is indeed immortal. Among the things that are spoken of are the fallibility of the senses, which leads to deception, and the nature of truth. It is shown in the course of a lengthy reasoning process that truth exists even in the midst of deception and falsehood (II, 5, 8 — 11, 20), and that, paradoxically, it would continue to exist even if it should perish (II, 15, 28). The argument concludes when Augustine's reason convinces him that, since truth of its very nature cannot perish, neither can the subjects in which truth inheres. These subjects are two — God and the soul. Hence the soul is proved to be imperishable and immortal (II, 18, 32 — 19, 33).

Some questions remain, nonetheless, and still others need to be reexamined. These will be treated in the sequel, *The Immortality of the Soul*, and the final pages of the second book point to the discussion that will occur there (II, 19, 33 — 20, 36). The most important aspects of the matter have been dealt with, however, in the *Soliloquies*.

Two significant observations may be made about how Augustine handles the search for God and the soul. The first is that, whereas the *Soliloquies* touch upon the actual nature of the soul, by demonstrating that it is immortal, they do not in fact touch upon the nature of God, except as that nature is hinted at in the long opening prayer (I, 1, 2-6). Instead they propose the means whereby a successful search for God may be carried out — namely, the preparation of the searcher through a virtuous life. The second observation is that, when Augustine reflects on the soul in the *Soliloquies*, he is not reflecting on it in the way that moderns do. He is concerned with the soul not from the psychological but from the metaphysical perspective, not as the basis for the possibility of a relational existence but as a discreet entity subject to investigation in itself. The overriding preoccupation with the soul's immortality certainly makes the treatise dull fare for many modern readers, but it was Augustine's conviction that this issue had to be resolved to his satisfaction before the soul could be spoken of meaningfully in any other way, as knowing and as capable of happiness. For him, moreover, as a recent (and as yet unbaptized) convert to Christianity, the issue perhaps had a freshness that it would not have had for others.

In addition to their philosophical content, the *Soliloquies* also provide interesting autobiographical information. They reveal, among other things, how important friendship was to him (I, 2, 7; I, 9, 16; I, 12, 20); his indifference to food (I, 3, 8; I, 10, 17); that he was afflicted by a terrible toothache (I, 12, 21), and that it had an adverse effect on his ability to write (I, 1, 1); that, while he may have put the idea of marriage and sexual gratification out of his thoughts (I, 10, 17 — 11, 18), he was still fascinated, perhaps even to an extent unknown to himself, by feminine beauty (I, 13, 22-23); and his reverence for Ambrose, who had played an important role in his conversion (II, 14, 26). In particular, the passage (I, 10, 17 — 12, 21) is one that gives considerable insight into Augustine's overall situation at the time of the writing of the *Soliloquies*. Of course, to a greater or a lesser degree, the treatise taken as a whole provides insight along that line as well.

Finally, the *Soliloquies* early on raise themes that will occupy Augustine for the rest of his life. Three or four of these have already been mentioned — namely, a systematic and methodical approach to problems, a deep interiority, a sense of quiet, a sense of yearning. There could also be mentioned in this context a certain facility of self-disclosure, as the previous paragraph suggests; a tendency toward theocentrism rather than christocentrism (I, 1, 2-6); an inclination to reduce matters to their most basic elements, as exemplified perfectly in the famous statement on desiring to know only God and the soul (I, 2, 7); a radical willingness to see everything in the light of the single object of one's desire, here expressed as wisdom (I, 11, 19 — 13, 23); a fascination with truth (I, 15, 27-29, *passim*); an emphasis on the immutability of God (II, 1, 1).

The *Soliloquies*, then, are valuable on a number of counts, and even if they do not achieve the majesty of Augustine's later works, there is at least an inkling here of the genius to come.

Boniface Ramsey, O.P.

Translator's Preface

Every translator states that he or she has tried to balance readability with a concern for literalness, and claims to have succeeded to one extent or another. My claims to such success are made very modestly: I can only state that I acknowledge the dilemma and have kept it in mind throughout my work, with perhaps a preference toward producing a smooth and readable English translation, with an economy of words.

If my translation represents an improvement over others, it is in a slight modernizing of the language for future readers. I have not used "Thou," "Thee," or "Thy," and have also avoided the vocative "O." I have been sparing in my capitalization of abstract nouns and titles. Perhaps most importantly, I have tried to pursue what I think is now the middle road on gender inclusive language. I have not used "man" or "mankind" when referring to all of humanity. I have avoided the generic "he," except when I thought that the original meaning would be violated or the flow of the passage ruined by circumlocutions, for example, "anyone who has come to know himself" (1, 4), not "anyone who has come to know him/herself," and certainly not the plural when a singular is meant, "anyone who has come to know themselves," a grammatically incorrect solution now endorsed by some.

Finally, I have tried to render terms neutrally when it seems that the original meaning would not be violated, for example, "country" rather than "fatherland," but have not done so when the gender seems intrinsic to the original meaning, especially when they are in reference to God, for example, "God, my king, my father" (I, 1, 4), not "Deity, my ruler, my parent."

I would like to thank all of my many language teachers, who at different times over the past fourteen years have tried their best to shape my often undisciplined mind. Special recognition should be given to my Latin teacher, Beverly Kinzle of Harvard Divinity School. Also, the professors with whom I have studied Augustine — John Cavadini of the University of Notre Dame, and David Townsend and Brother Robert Smith of St. John's College — are three of the finest teachers I have had the good fortune of knowing. The enthusiasm they have for the material they teach has inspired many students.

My love and gratitude go out to my wife for living with me during the trials of graduate school. To my father and to the memory of my mother, my first and best teachers, who instilled in me an abiding curiosity and love for learning and tradition, I dedicate this work of translation.

Kim Paffenroth

Soliloquies

Book I

Purpose

1, 1. For a long time I had been turning over in my mind many diverse things; for many days I had been diligently searching for myself and my own good, and for what evil should be avoided, when suddenly someone spoke to me. Whether it was I myself or someone else, whether it was outside of me or within me, I just do not know, no matter how hard I try to figure it out. This is what he said to me —

Reason: Now look here: suppose you had discovered something; into whose care would you put it, so that you could get on with other things?

Augustine: To memory, certainly.

Reason: Oh? Is memory so great that it can accurately hold on to everything that has been conceived?

Augustine: That is difficult to do; indeed, it is impossible.

Reason: Therefore it must be written down. But what do you do when your health will not let you write?[1] These things ought not to be dictated, for they need complete privacy.

Augustine: What you say is true. Indeed, I do not know what I would do.

Reason: Pray for good health and aid, so that you may accomplish what you desire; and put it in writing, so that your confidence may be increased by what you have done. Then briefly summarize your discovery in a few short conclusions. But you should not bother about attracting a lot of readers: this will be enough for a few of your fellow citizens.

Augustine: I will do just that.

Prayer

2. God, founder of the universe, first grant to me that I might rightly beseech you; then let me act as one worthy of being heard, so that finally you might set me free.

You are God, through whom all things, which by themselves would not exist, strive to exist; God, who does not let even self-destructive things perish; God, who from nothing has made this world, which all eyes judge to be most beautiful; God, who does not make evil, and even prevents what is evil from becoming the worst evil; God, who reveals, to the few who take refuge in that which truly is, that evil is nothing; God, because of whom the universe is perfect, even with its imperfections; God, because of whom even the most extreme dissonance no longer exists, since inferior things harmonize with the superior; God, who is loved by everything which is capable of loving, whether they do it knowingly or unknowingly; God, in whom are all things, but who is neither corrupted by the corruption of all creation, nor hurt by its evil, nor deceived by its error; God, who has wanted only the pure to know what is true.[2] You are God, father of truth, father of wisdom, father of true and complete life, father of blessedness, father of goodness and beauty, father of intelligible light, father of our awakening and enlightenment, father of the assurance which admonishes us to return to you.

3. I call upon you, God, truth, in whom and by whom and through whom all true things are true; God, wisdom, in whom and by whom and through whom all the wise are wise; God, true and complete life, in whom and by whom and through whom lives all that is truly and completely alive; God, blessedness, in whom and by whom and through whom all blessed things are blessed; God, goodness and beauty, in whom and by whom and through whom all good and beautiful things are good and beautiful; God, intelligible light, in whom and by whom and through whom all things which give off intelligible light have intelligible light; God, whose realm is that entire world which perception does not know; God, from whose realm the law is transposed even on to these realms; God, from whom to turn away is to fall, to whom to turn toward is to rise again, in whom to remain is to stand firm; God, from whom to go away is to die, to whom to return is to be alive again, in whom to dwell is to live; God, whom no one loses unless deceived, whom no one seeks unless admonished, whom no one finds unless cleansed; God, whom to forsake is to perish, whom to follow is to love, whom to see is to have; God, to whom faith calls us, hope encourages us, love unites us; God, through whom we overcome the enemy, I entreat you.

God, through whom we receive, that we might not perish utterly; God, by whom we are admonished, so that we might be watchful; God, through whom we separate good from evil; God, through whom we avoid evil and pursue good; God, through whom we do not yield to misfortunes; God, through whom we rightly serve and rightly rule; God, through whom we learn that what we once considered ours is in fact not our own, but what we once considered not our own is in fact ours; God, through whom we do not hang on to the baits and lures of evil things; God, through whom petty things do not diminish us; God, through whom what is superior in us is not subjugated by what is inferior; God, through whom *death is swallowed up in victory* (1 Cor 15:54); God, who converts us; God, who strips off of us that which is not, and clothes us with that which is;[3] God, who makes us able to be heard; God, who strengthens us;[4] God, who leads us into every truth;[5] God, who tells us all good things, and neither drives us mad, nor allows anyone else to do so; God, who calls us back to the way;[6] God, who leads us to the door;[7] God, who causes it to be opened *for those who knock* (Mt 7:8); God who gives us *the bread of life* (Jn 6:35.48); God, through whom we thirst *for that drink which will make us thirst no more* (Jn 6:35); God, who *shows to the world sin, justice, and judgment* (Jn 16:8);[8] God, through whom we are not moved by those who do not believe; God, through whom we reject the error of those who think that souls are neither praised nor blamed by you; God, through whom we do not serve *weak and destitute elements* (Gal 4:9); God, who cleanses us and prepares us for divine rewards, gracious God, come to me.

4. In all that has been said by me, you are the one God; come now to my aid, you who are the one, eternal, true substance, in which there is no conflict, no confusion, no change, no want, no death; in which there is perfect harmony, perfect clarity, perfect stability, perfect abundance, perfect life; in which there is nothing lacking and nothing superfluous; in which the *one who begets and the one who is begotten is one* (Jn 10:30).[9]

God, who is served by everything which serves and who is submitted to by every good soul; God, by whose laws the axes revolve, the celestial bodies complete their courses, the sun rules the day, the moon governs the night, and the whole world (insofar as perceptible matter allows) maintains the great stability of things by the ordering and repetition of times, through the days by the alternation of light and darkness, through the months by the waxing and waning of the moon, through the years by the successions of spring, summer, fall, and winter, through the periods by the completion of the course of the sun, through the great cycles by return of the celestial bodies to their original places;[10] God, by whose eternally established laws the irregular motion of changeable things is not allowed to be completely disordered, but is always called back to a semblance of stability by the restraints of the surrounding ages; God, by whose laws the soul has free will, and the rewards of the good and the punishments of the evil are assigned by a necessity which has been established for all; God, from whom all good things flow to us, and by whom all evil things are diverted from us; God, over whom there is nothing, outside of whom there is nothing, and without whom there is nothing; God, under whom is everything, in whom is everything, and with whom is everything; God, who has made humanity in your *image and likeness* (Gn 1:26), which anyone who has come to know himself recognizes: listen, listen, listen to me, my God, my lord, my king, my father, my cause, my hope, my treasure, my honor, my home, my country, my salvation, my life, listen, listen, listen to me in that way of yours known only to a few.

5. Now I love only you, I follow only you, I seek for only you, and I am ready to serve only you, because only you justly govern; I long to be under your rule. Command me, I beg you, and make any decree you wish, but heal and open my ears, so that I may hear your voice. Heal and open my eyes, so that I may see what is your will. Drive my madness from me, so that I may know you again. Tell me where I

should look, so that I may see you; I hope to do all which you have commanded. Take back, I entreat you, your rebellious servant, my lord, most merciful father. By now I have suffered enough punishments, I have been enslaved long enough by your enemies, whom you have under your feet, I have been battered long enough by lies. Take back your servant as I flee from these things, even as they took me in as a foreign guest when I fled from you. I know I must return to you; let your door be open to my knocking;[11] show me how to reach you. I have nothing except my will, I know nothing else except that the unstable and perishable should be shunned, while the sure and eternal should be pursued. I do this, father, because I know only this; but how to reach you, I do not know. Push me forward, show me the way, and give me provisions for the journey. If those who flee to you find you by faith, then give me faith; if by virtue, then give me virtue; if by knowledge, then give me knowledge. Give me more faith, more hope, more love.[12] How astonishing and unique is your goodness!

6. I come to you for the very things whereby an approach can be made to you, so that I might beseech you again. For the one whom you abandon is lost forever. But you do not abandon anyone, for you are the perfect good, which no one has rightly searched for and not found. All those who rightly search for you, you have caused to search rightly for you. Make me, father, search for you, protect me from evil; and as I search, let there be nothing else for me other than you, I beg you, father. If there is in me a desire for anything that would weigh me down, rid me of it yourself and make me fit to see you. As for all that has to do with the health of my mortal body, since I do not know what is useful to me or my loved ones, I entrust it to you, wisest and best father, and I will only ask for it what you suggest at the time. I only

pray for your most excellent mercy, so that you may convert me completely to you, allowing nothing to be in my way as I approach you; and as long as I possess and carry around this body, command me to be pure, generous, just, and prudent, a perfect lover and student of your wisdom, worthy of a home, even of a home in your most blessed realm. Amen, amen.

I want to know God and the soul

2, 7. *Augustine:* There, I have prayed to God.

Reason: What then do you wish to know?

Augustine: All the things for which I prayed.

Reason: Summarize them briefly.

Augustine: I want to know God and the soul.[13]

Reason: Nothing more?

Augustine: Nothing whatsoever.

Reason: Then begin to search. But first explain how God could be shown to you, so that you would be able to say, "That is enough."

Augustine: I do not know how God could be shown to me so that I would say, "That is enough." For I do not think that I know anything in the way that I wish to know God.

Reason: How then are we to proceed? Do you not think that first you should know how you could know God satisfactorily, so that when you reach that point you will not search more?

Augustine: I do think so, but I do not see how it can be done. For what thing similar to God have I ever understood in such a way that I could say, "I want to understand God in the same way that I understand this"?

Reason: But you do not know God yet, so how do you know that you know nothing similar to God?

Augustine: Because if I were to know something similar to God, without a doubt I would love it. But now I love nothing other than God and the soul, and I know neither of them.

Reason: Then do you not love your friends?[14]

Augustine: How could I love the soul, but not love them?

Reason: Do you therefore love even fleas and bugs?

Augustine: I said I love the soul, not everything that has a soul.[15]

Reason: Then either you do not have human beings for friends, or else you do not love them; for every human being is a creature with a soul, and you said that you do not love creatures with souls.

Augustine: They are indeed human beings and I do love them, though not because they are creatures with souls, but because they are human, which is to say that they have rational souls, which I love even in criminals. For I can love reason in anyone, even though I justly hate the one who wrongly uses that which I love. And therefore I love my friends all the more, the more they use the rational soul well, or at least inasmuch as they wish to use it well.

How much I want to know God

3, 8. *Reason:* I accept that. But nonetheless, if someone said to you, "I will make you know God in the same way that you know Alypius," would not you thank him and say, "That is enough"?[16]

Augustine: I would indeed thank him, but I would not say that it was enough.

Reason: Why, I would like to know?

Augustine: Because I do not know God as well as I do Alypius, and even Alypius I do not know sufficiently.

Reason: Be careful: it may be impudent to want to know God sufficiently, when you do not even know Alypius sufficiently.

Augustine: That does not follow. For in comparison to the celestial bodies, what is more worthless than my dinner? And yet I do not know what I will have for dinner tomorrow, but without impudence I claim to know in what sign the moon will be.

Reason: Therefore it is enough for you if you know God as you know in what sign the moon will run its course tomorrow?

Augustine: That is not enough. For I believe in the latter based on the senses. But I do not know whether God or some hidden natural cause may suddenly alter the regularity and course of the moon. And if that happened, all my presuppositions would prove false.

Reason: And do you believe that this is possible?

Augustine: I do not believe so. But I am searching for what I can know, not just what I can believe. For it is said, perhaps rightly, that we believe everything we know, but not that we know everything we believe.

Reason: Therefore you reject, in this case, all the evidence of the senses?

Augustine: I reject it completely.[17]

Reason: What about that friend of yours, whom you say you still do not know, do you wish to know him by sense or by the intellect?

Augustine: What I know of him by sense, if indeed anything can be known by sense, is worthless, and I have had enough of it. But that part of him that makes him my friend, that is to say his soul, I want to grasp by the intellect.

Reason: Can it be known in any other way?

Augustine: In no other way.

Reason: Then you dare to say that your friend and intimate acquaintance is unknown to you?

Augustine: Why should I not dare? For it is thought to be most just that the law of friendship commands that *one love a friend neither less nor more than oneself* (Lv 19:18). Therefore, since I do not know myself, how can it be held against me if I say that someone is unknown to me, especially when, as I believe, he does not know himself?

Reason: Then the things which you want to know are of the class of things which the intellect grasps; therefore, when I said that it was impudent of you to want to know God when you did not know Alypius, you should not have made the comparison of your dinner and the moon, if these, as you said, belong to the senses.

What does it mean to know God?

4, 9. But that is not important. Now answer this: if the things which Plato and Plotinus said about God are true, is it enough for you to know God as they did?[18]

Augustine: It does not necessarily follow that if the things they said were true, then they knew them. For many people talk a lot about things they do not know, just as I said I wanted to know all the things for which I prayed; but I would not want them, if I already knew them. Did that make me speak less about them? No, for I spoke not of the things which I understand with my intellect, but of those things which I had gathered from various places and entrusted to memory; I had as much faith in them as I could. But to know something, that is entirely different.

Reason: Tell me, please, do you at least know what a line is in geometry?

Augustine: I know that clearly.

Reason: And in saying this you are not afraid of the Skeptics?[19]

Augustine: Not at all. For they say that a wise person cannot make a mistake, but I am not wise. Therefore I am not afraid to claim knowledge of the things I know. And if I fulfill my desire of reaching wisdom, I will do what it tells me.

Reason: I see nothing wrong in that. But what I had begun to ask was whether you know a ball, which is called a sphere, just as you know a line.

Augustine: I do.

Reason: Do you know them both equally, or one more or less than the other?

Augustine: Both equally. I make no mistakes in either case.

Reason: And did you perceive these by the senses or by the intellect?

Augustine: In this case I have used the senses like a ship.[20] For when they had carried me to my destination and I had left them, and I was placed, as it were, on dry land, I began to turn these things over in my thoughts, but my steps were for a long time uncertain. So it seems to me that one could sail a ship on dry land more easily than one could perceive geometry by the senses, even though they do seem to help those who are first learning.

Reason: Then whatever instruction you have had in these things, you do not hesitate to call that knowledge?

Augustine: No, if the Stoics would allow it, for they attribute knowledge to no one who is not wise. I do not deny that I have an understanding of these things, which they admit that even fools can have. But I am not afraid of them. So these things about which you asked, I say I possess them as knowledge. But proceed: I want to see why you are asking these questions.

Reason: Do not rush: we are in no hurry. Just pay close attention, so that you do not concede a point carelessly. I am eager to give you peace of mind about some things which from now on will give you no more trouble; do you still want me to hurry on, as if it were an insignificant matter?

Augustine: May God make it as you have described it. Question me as you please and rebuke me more severely if I act that way again.

10. *Reason:* Therefore it is clear to you that splitting a line in two lengthwise is absolutely impossible?

Augustine: That is clear.

Reason: What about crosswise?

Augustine: It can be cut crosswise an infinite number of times.

Reason: What about a sphere? Is it equally clear that having cut a sphere through its center, there will be no two equal circles in either one of the halves?

Augustine: That is equally clear.

Reason: So, do the line and the sphere seem to you to be one thing, or do they differ from one another in some way?

Augustine: Who could not see that they differ in many ways?

Reason: But if you know both one and the other equally, and yet you admit that they differ from one another in many ways, then is there a single, undifferentiated knowledge of things that are different?

Augustine: Who would say that there is not?

Reason: You did, just a little while ago. For when I asked you how you want to know God so that you could say, "That is enough," you replied that you could not explain that, because you have never perceived anything in the way in which you wish to perceive God, for you know nothing that is like God. Well, what now? Are the line and the sphere alike?[21]

Augustine: Who would say that?

Reason: But I was not asking what things you know that are like God, but rather, what things you know as you wish to know God. For you know the line just as you know the sphere, even though the line and the sphere are very different. So tell me whether it would be enough for you to know God as you know this geometric sphere, so that you would have no uncertainty about God, just as you have none about the sphere.

Differences

5, 11. *Augustine:* Excuse me, but no matter how hard you push me and try to show me my error, I still do not dare to say that I wish to know God as I know these things. For it seems to me that not only the objects are different, but even the knowledge itself. First, the line and the sphere are not so different from one another, for one type of learning can contain them both. But no geometry expert has ever claimed to teach knowledge of God. Secondly, if the knowledge of God and of these things were the same, then knowing them would make me rejoice as much as I expect to rejoice in knowing God. But now in comparison to God I look down on these things so much that it sometimes seems to me that if I ever know and see God in the way in which

God can be seen, then all these things will disappear from my thoughts; even now, because of my love for God, they hardly enter my mind.

Reason: You will indeed rejoice more, much more, in knowing God than in knowing these things, but it is the objects that differ, not the way of knowing them; unless you think that you look at the earth with one type of vision and at the clear sky with another, even though the sight of the latter is much more pleasing to you. But unless your eyes are deceived, I believe that if you were asked whether you see the earth as surely as you see the sky, you would have to answer that it is just as certain, even though you rejoice in the beauty and splendor of the sky, and not so much in the earth.

Augustine: I must admit that comparison persuades me and leads me to agree that as the earth differs from the sky, so too the true and certain proofs of the sciences differ from the intelligible majesty of God.

The purified mind and contemplation

6, 12. *Reason:* You are right to be persuaded. For Reason, who is speaking to you, promises to show to your mind just as the sun is shown to your eyes. For the senses of the soul are like the eyes of the mind;[22] those things which are most certain in the sciences are like the things illuminated by the sun so that they can be seen, such as the earth and everything on it. But now it is God who illuminates. I am Reason; I am to minds as sight is to the eyes. For having eyes is not the same as looking, and looking is not the same as seeing.[23] Therefore the soul needs three things: it must have eyes which it can use properly, then it must look, then it must see. To have healthy eyes is to have a mind cleansed of every stain of the body, that is, a mind purified and free from all the lusts for mortal things. And at first, nothing other than faith can give this. For if one's mind is corrupted and sickened by defects, then no one can show it that the mind cannot see unless it is healthy; and if the mind does not believe that otherwise it cannot see, then it will make no attempt to improve its health. But if it believes that the matter is as I have described it, and that when it can see it will see, nonetheless the mind despairs of ever being cured. Will it not then give up completely and despise itself, and not obey the doctor's orders?

Augustine: That is certainly true, especially since the person who is ill must experience the treatment as harsh.

Reason: Therefore hope must be added to faith.

Augustine: So I believe.

Reason: But if the mind believes that things are this way and hopes that it can be cured, but does not yet love nor desire the promised light, then it will think that it ought to be content with the darkness, which is pleasant because the mind is used to it. Would not the mind then still reject the doctor?

Augustine: That is certainly so.

Reason: Therefore the third requirement is love.

Augustine: There is nothing which is so necessary.[24]

Reason: Therefore, without these three things no soul can be cured so that it can see, that is, understand its God.

13. And once it has healthy eyes, what else is required?

Augustine: That it look.

Reason: The soul's vision is reason. But since it does not follow that looking always results in seeing, the right and perfect looking which results in seeing is called virtue; for virtue is right or perfect reason. But looking by itself cannot turn even healthy eyes toward the light, unless these three things remain: faith, by which one believes that the thing looked at will make one blessed when it is seen; hope, by which one expects to see, once one has looked well; love, by which one desires to see and to enjoy. After looking, one sees God, which therefore ends the looking, not because it no longer exists, but because it has nothing more toward which to strive. And this is truly perfect virtue, reason attaining its goal, which results in a blessed life. But the seeing itself is that understanding which is in the soul and which is brought about by the one who understands and that which is understood, just as what is called seeing in the eyes consists of sensing and what is sensed, and if either of these is missing, nothing can be seen.

Vision

7, 14. Therefore, when the soul has seen God, that is, understood God, let us see whether these three things are still necessary. Why should faith be necessary, when one already sees? Or hope, when one already has the object? But as for love, not only will nothing be taken away from it, but even more will be added. For when the soul sees that unique and true beauty, it will love it more; but unless it will fix its eye with boundless love and not turn from looking, it will not be able to remain in that blessed vision. But as long as the soul is in the body, even if it can most fully see, that is, understand God, this is nevertheless the case: that since the senses of the body are operating normally, and although they cannot deceive, they do tend to be uncertain, and therefore faith can be called that by which the soul doubts the senses and believes something else to be true.

Similarly, even though in this life the soul is blessed by its understanding of God,[25] nevertheless it endures many bodily distractions, and therefore it needs the hope that all these troubles will not exist after death. Therefore hope does not abandon the soul in this life. But after this life, when the soul has brought itself completely to God, love will remain and hold it there. For it cannot be said to have faith that these things are true, when it is no longer bothered by any disturbance of falsehood; nor is there anything left to hope for, since it securely possesses everything. Therefore, three things are important to the soul: that it be healthy, that it look, and that it see. And another three, faith, hope, and love, are always necessary for health and looking; as for seeing, in this life all three are necessary for it, but after this life only love is necessary.

Illumination

8, 15. Now understand, insofar as the present situation requires, something about God which I will now show you from a comparison with sensible things. For God is intelligible, as the observations of the sciences are intelligible; nevertheless they differ greatly. For both the earth and light are visible, but the earth cannot be seen unless it is illuminated by light. Likewise, those things which are taught by the sciences and which anyone with understanding unreservedly acknowledges as completely true cannot be understood unless they are illuminated by something like their own sun. For just as in the sun one can perceive three things — that it is, that it shines, and that it illuminates — so too in that most hidden God whom you wish to understand, there are three things — that he is, that he can be understood, and that he makes it possible to understand other things. I dare to teach you these two things, yourself and God, so that you may understand them. But tell me, how would you receive these, as probable or as true?

Augustine: Certainly, only as probable, though I must confess that I had fostered a greater hope; for besides those two objects, the line and the sphere, there is nothing in what you have said which I would dare to say that I know.

Reason: That is not remarkable, for I have not yet explained anything enough that it would demand assent from you.

Are we healthy?

9, 16. But why do we delay? We should be on our way. The first question before all others is to see whether we are healthy.

Augustine: You will see the answer to that, if you can at all look into yourself or me. I will answer your questions, if I notice anything.

Reason: Do you love anything other than the knowledge of yourself and God?

Augustine: I could answer that I love nothing else, if I followed my present feelings; but it would be more cautious for me to say that I do not know. For it has often happened to me that just when I thought nothing else could upset me, something nevertheless came into my mind which bothered me much more than I had anticipated. Likewise, although something may not have struck me at all when it entered my mind, yet when it really happened, it disturbed me more than I had expected. But right now it seems to me that I could be upset by only three things: fear of losing those whom I love, fear of pain, and fear of death.

Reason: Therefore you love living with your dearest friends, and your good health, and also your life itself in this body; for otherwise you would not fear losing these things.

Augustine: I admit that is so.

Reason: Right now, therefore, since all your friends are not with you and your health is less than perfect, your soul must be a little troubled; I think that must be the result.

Augustine: You are quite right; I cannot deny it.

Reason: But what if you suddenly felt and were assured that you had bodily health, and you were to see all those whom you love peacefully enjoying ease and leisure, would it not bring you some joy?

Augustine: Yes indeed, a certain amount; especially if, as you say, these things were to happen suddenly, how could I contain myself, how could I be allowed to hide that kind of delight?

Reason: So you would still be troubled by all the diseases and disturbances of the soul. Is it not somewhat impudent, then, for such eyes to wish to see that sun?

Augustine: You have concluded this as though I have not really improved my health, and do not know which of my ills have disappeared and which remain. You must admit that is true.

Various pleasures

10, 17. *Reason:* But do you not see that these bodily eyes, even when healthy, are often repelled and turned away from the light of this sun, fleeing back into their own darkness? But you are thinking of your progress, without thinking about what you wish to see; nevertheless, I will talk with you about this, about what progress you think we have made. Do you have no desire for riches?[26]

Augustine: No, and this is not the first time I have said so. For I am thirty-three years old, and it has been fourteen years since I stopped desiring riches. And if they happened to be offered to me, I only thought of them as providing for the necessities of life, and of their generous use. Just one book of Cicero easily persuaded me that riches are in no way to be pursued, and if they just happen to come along, they should be managed most wisely and cautiously.[27]

Reason: What about honors?

Augustine: I admit that only in these last few days have I stopped desiring them.[28]

Reason: What about a wife? Would not it be nice sometimes to have a beautiful, modest, compliant woman, one who is well-read or whom you could easily teach, one without too much of a dowry, because you hate riches, but with enough that she would not be bothersome to your leisure; would that not be nice, especially if you hoped and were even sure that you would have no trouble from her?

Augustine: However much you wish to embellish her and to pile on every good quality, I have decided that there is nothing I should avoid as much as sex. For I know of nothing that so debases a man's soul as the charms of a woman and that bodily contact which is so much a part of having a wife. Therefore — and this is not yet settled for me — if it is the duty of a wise man to take care of children, then anyone who has sex for this reason alone is seen by me as admirable, but certainly not to be imitated. For the danger in such an attempt is greater than the happiness to be gained by it. For this reason I believe it is fair, just, and useful for the freedom of my soul that I have commanded myself not to desire, not to seek, and not to marry a wife.[29]

Reason: I am not now asking what you have decided, but whether you are still struggling with your lust, or whether you have truly defeated it. For this is about the health of your eyes.

Augustine: I am not at all seeking anything of that kind, nor do I desire it; it is only with fear and contempt that I even recall it. What more do you want? And this good feeling grows stronger in me daily, for the more the hope increases of seeing that beauty which I so ardently long for, the more all my love and joy are turned toward it.

Reason: What about the pleasure of eating? How much is that worth to you?[30]

Augustine: Those things which I have decided not to eat do not disturb me at all. I admit that those things which I have not cut out do attract me when they are in front of me, but only in such a way that even if I had seen and tasted them, they could be taken away without any disturbance to my soul. And when they are not there, the appetite for them does not dare come as an interference into my thoughts. But in all this, you need not ask about food or drink or bathing or any other bodily pleasure: I seek to have just enough of them as can contribute to my health.

Justice

11. 18. *Reason:* You have made much progress. Nevertheless, those things which remain can still very much hinder your seeing that light. What I am getting at — and it seems to me easily demonstrated — is that either nothing remains for us to overcome, or that we have made no progress at all, and all the rottenness of those things which we thought we had cut out in fact remains. I ask you this: if you were

convinced that you could not live with your many dear
friends in pursuit of wisdom unless there was great wealth
to provide for your regular needs, would you not want and
wish for riches?

Augustine: I would.

Reason: And what if it happened that you could convince
many people to pursue wisdom, if only your prestige were
increased by honors; and what if your friends could not
control their desires and turn completely to seeking God
unless they also were given honors, which would not be
possible except through your honors and rank; would not
these things then be desirable, and would you not eagerly
pursue acquiring them?

Augustine: It is as you say.

Reason: I will not argue about a wife, for it may be that
there is no necessity of marrying one. But what if it were
certain that her great wealth could support all those whom
you wish to have living peacefully with you in one place,
while she herself would be in complete agreement with this;
and what if she were so powerful because of her aristocratic
family that through her you could easily get those honors
which you have already conceded to be necessary; if all this
were true, I am not so sure that it would be your duty to
despise all this, are you?

Augustine: But how could I dare to hope for all that?

19. *Reason:* You talk as if I were now asking about what
you hope for. I am not asking about what does not give you
pleasure when it is absent, but about what does give you
pleasure when it is available. For it is one thing for a disease
to be eradicated, and quite another for it merely to be in
remission. In regard to this, it is worth noting what some
learned men have said: all fools are mad, just as all filth
smells bad, although you do not notice it all the time, but

only when you stir it up.[31] There is a great difference between burying a desire because of the soul's desperation, and really driving it out with good health.

Augustine: Although I cannot answer you, you still will never persuade me to believe that I have made no progress, when I know in what kind of mental state I am now.

Reason: I believe it seems this way to you because, although you might want these things, they nevertheless seem desirable not for their own sakes, but for the sake of something else.

Augustine: That is what I wanted to say. For when I used to desire riches, I desired them just in order to be rich; and those honors, the longing for which I said that I have only recently subdued, I wanted them because I was delighted by a certain brilliance about them; and when I was looking for a wife, I never looked for anything other than that she would bring me pleasure and good repute. At that time there was a real desire in me for these things, but now I despise them all. But if it is only through these things that I can find a way to the things which I now want, then I pursue them not as things to be embraced, but I submit to them as things to be endured.

Reason: Very well, for I do not think it can be called a desire, if the things are only wanted for the sake of something else.

Search for ourselves and for God

12, 20. But I ask you, why do you want those people whom you love to live, or more specifically, to live with you?

Augustine: So that together and in complete agreement we can search for ourselves and God. For in that way, whoever first makes a discovery can easily lead the others to it without difficulty.

Reason: But what if they do not want to search for these things?

Augustine: I will convince them, so that they will want to.

Reason: But what if you are unable to do that, either because they have decided that these things are already found, or are impossible to find, or because they are hindered by cares and desires for other things?

Augustine: I will teach them, and they me, as much as we can.[32]

Reason: But what if their very presence keeps you from your search? Would not this trouble you and, if they cannot change, make you wish that they were not with you, rather than be like this?

Augustine: I admit it is as you say.

Reason: Therefore you do not desire their life or their presence for its own sake, but only in order to find wisdom?

Augustine: I agree completely.

Reason: What if you were certain that your life itself was keeping you from reaching wisdom, would you wish it to continue?

Augustine: I would flee from it in every way.

Reason: What if you were shown that you could arrive at wisdom, whether you left this body or remained in it, would you then care whether it were in this life or another that you obtained the object of your love?

Augustine: As long as I knew that I would experience nothing worse which would drive me back from the point to which I have come, I would not care.

Reason: Therefore you now fear death, because you might be taken by a worse evil, which would deprive you of knowledge of the divine?

Augustine: Not only do I fear that I would be deprived of what I might have learned already, but that I would be hindered from approaching those things which I still long to learn; but I do believe that what I now know will remain with me.

Reason: Therefore, you wish this life to continue, not for its own sake, but for the sake of wisdom?

Augustine: That is so.

21. *Reason:* There remains bodily pain, which might disturb you with its power.

Augustine: I dread that a great deal, though not in itself, but because it might keep me from my search. For the past few days I have been tormented by a most piercing tooth-ache,[33] such that I contemplated in my mind nothing except what I had already learned; I was completely prevented from learning anything, because that requires total concentration of the mind. Nevertheless, it seemed to me that if the light of truth had been revealed to my mind, I either would not have felt that pain, or would have endured it as if it were nothing. And although I myself have never suffered anything worse, nevertheless I often think of how many worse things could happen, so that I am forced some-times to agree with Cornelius Celsus,[34] who says that the greatest good is wisdom, and the greatest evil is bodily pain. Nor does his reasoning seem ridiculous to me. For he says, "We are composed of two parts, soul and body; the first is the better, while the body is the inferior; so the greatest good is what is best in the superior part, while the greatest evil is what is worst in the inferior part. Wisdom is the best thing in the soul, while pain is the worst thing in the body." So it may be concluded without error, I think, that the greatest human good is to be wise, and the greatest evil is to feel pain.

Reason: We will see about that later. For perhaps the wisdom which we are trying to find will convince us otherwise. But if wisdom will show that this is true, then we will hold on to this definition of the greatest good and the greatest evil without any doubt.

Lover of wisdom

13, 22. Now let us ask about what sort of lover of wisdom you are: you long to see and to hold her, with a most pure gaze and in an embrace that has no veil in between, naked as it were, in a way that she allows to only a few and most select of her lovers. Now if you burned with love for some beautiful woman, would she not be right not to give herself to you, if she found that you loved something besides her? So how can the purest beauty of wisdom show herself to you, unless you are ablaze for her alone?

Augustine: Why am I held back by this unhappiness and delayed by this miserable torment? Surely I have shown that I love nothing else, for anything which is not loved for its own sake is not really loved. I love only wisdom for her own sake, and only for her sake do I want to have, and fear losing, other things, such as life, peace, friends. How can my love of that beauty have a limit? Not only do I not begrudge her to others, but I even seek many more who will pursue her with me, long for her with me, grasp her with me, and enjoy her with me, and they will be my friends even more, the more the love of her is shared among us.

23. *Reason:* That is just how lovers of wisdom ought to be. She seeks such lovers, whose union with her is completely pure and without any defilement. But there is not just one way to her.[35] Indeed, each one seizes that unique and truest

good, according to his or her own strength. It is a mental light, indescribable and incomprehensible. The ordinary light shows, as much as it can, what that other one is like. For some eyes are so healthy and vigorous that as soon as they open, they turn toward the sun itself without any fear. For these, light itself is health,[36] and they do not need a teacher, but only perhaps some guidance. For these, believing, hoping, and loving are enough. But there are others who fervently wish to see the light, but are so struck by its brilliance that they often turn back with gladness to the darkness without having seen the light. Even though they can rightly be called healthy, it is dangerous to wish to show them what they cannot yet see. Therefore they must be trained first, and for their own good their love must be directed and nurtured. First they should be shown things which do not have their own light, but which can be seen by light, such as a cloth or a wall or something like that. Then there are those things which do not shine by themselves, although they sparkle more beautifully in that light, such as gold, silver, and the like, but which do not shine so much as to hurt the eyes. Then perhaps this earthly fire can be shown to them, then the stars, then the moon, then the brilliance of the dawn and the radiance of the brightening sky. Whether one does it quickly or slowly, going through all the stages or omitting some, growing accustomed to them according to his or her own strength, it is through these things that one will see the sun without fear and with great joy. The best teachers do something like this with those who are most eager for wisdom, those who can see, though not yet clearly. For it is the duty of good teaching to reach it in an orderly manner; without order it would be a barely believable stroke of good luck.

But we have written enough for one day, I think; stopping now is for our health.

Cast off the things of the senses

14, 24. *(On the next day) Augustine:* I ask you, please give me that order, if you can now. Lead me, direct me, wherever you wish, by whatever means you wish, however you wish. Give me whatever difficult and strenuous tasks you like, as long as they are within my power, through which I may without doubt attain what I desire.

Reason: I can give you only one piece of advice, I do not know any more: these things of the senses must be completely cast off.[37] We must take great care, as long as we are in this body, that our wings do not become mired in the things of the senses, for we need complete and perfect wings to fly to that light from this darkness. That light does not deign to reveal itself to those trapped in this prison, unless they are able to break out of the prison and destroy it, and escape to their own higher places. So when you have become such a person that no earthly thing at all gives you pleasure, believe me, at that moment, at that exact point in time, you will see what you desire.

Augustine: But when will that be, I ask you? For I do not think that these things can become completely worthless to me, unless I see that thing in comparison to which these things are based.

25. *Reason:* If that's the case, then the eye of this body could say, "Only when I have seen the sun will I not love the darkness." This might also seem to be in agreement with order, but it is far from it. The eye loves the darkness because it is not healthy; it cannot see the sun unless it is

healthy. The soul is often mistaken in this way, thinking and claiming that it is healthy; and since it cannot see, the soul even thinks it right to complain. But that beauty knows when to reveal itself. It acts as a physician, knowing better who are the healthy ones than do those who are themselves being treated. We think we can see how far we have come; but we neither know nor feel how deeply we were immersed or what progress we have made. Therefore, in comparison with a worse disease we think ourselves healthy. Do you not know how confidently yesterday we declared ourselves free of any affliction, lovers only of wisdom, seeking and desiring other things only for its sake? A woman's embrace seemed to you so base, so foul, so despicable, so disgusting, when we inquired into the desire for a wife. But that night, lying awake and going back over those things,[38] you realized that those imagined charms and bitter sweetness excited you much differently than you had anticipated; much, much less than usual, but also much differently than you had thought. That most hidden physician showed you both what you had escaped by his treatment, as well as what remains to be treated.

14. 26. *Augustine:* Be silent, I beg you, be silent. Why do you torment me? Why do you probe and pierce so deeply? Now I cannot keep from crying; from now on I will promise nothing, I will take nothing for granted, only do not ask me about these things. You say that the one whom I long to see will know when I am healthy. Let him do what he pleases; when it pleases him, let him reveal himself. I now give myself entirely to his mercy and care. I have always believed that he does not hesitate to help those who are turned toward him. Until I see that beauty, I will say nothing about my health.

Reason: Do nothing other than that. But now stop your tears and compose yourself. You have certainly cried a great deal, and that surely worsens your chest-illness.

Augustine: You wish my tears to end, when I can see no end to my misery? Or do you command me to take care of my bodily health, when my inmost health is wasting away with disease? But I beg you, if you have some power over me, try to lead me through whatever shortcuts you can. Through nearness to that light (which I can bear if I have made some progress), I will be ashamed to turn my eyes back to that darkness which I have abandoned (if indeed it can be called abandoned when it still tries to charm my blindness).

To know truth

15, 27. *Reason:* Let us finish this first book, if you please, so that we may begin the second in an appropriate way. For given your condition, you should not stop working with moderation.

Augustine: There is no way I will let this book be completed, unless you show me something about the nearness of the light toward which I am striving.

Reason: That physician bears with you. I do not know what beam guides and urges me on to where I am leading you, so listen carefully.

Augustine: Lead me, I beg you, and hurry on to wherever you wish.

Reason: You say with certainty that you wish to know God and the soul?

Augustine: That is my only concern.

Reason: Nothing more?

Augustine: Nothing whatsoever.

Reason: Do you not want to understand the truth?

Augustine: I could not know these things except by means of it.

Reason: Therefore it must first be known, and through it those other things can be known.

Augustine: I agree completely.

Reason: Let us first see this: "truth" and "true" are two words; does it therefore seem to you that two things are signified by these words, or just one?

Augustine: They seem to be two things. For just as "chastity" is one thing and "chaste" another (and there are many other examples like this), so I think that "truth" is one thing and what is called "true" is another.

Reason: Which of them do you think is better?

Augustine: Truth, I think. For just as chastity does not exist because someone is chaste, but rather someone is chaste because of chastity, likewise, if something is true, it is true because of truth.

15. 28. *Reason:* If some chaste person dies, do you think that chastity also dies?

Augustine: In no way.

Reason: Therefore, when something true disappears, truth does not disappear.

Augustine: How could something true disappear? I do not see that.

Reason: I wonder how you could ask that. Do we not see thousands of things disappear before our eyes? Perhaps you think that this tree is a tree, but not a true tree, or that it cannot possibly disappear? For even if you did not believe the senses and could answer that you do not know whether it is really a tree, nevertheless you will not, I think, deny that if it is indeed a tree, it is a true tree. For this is a judgment of intellect, not of sense. If it is a false tree, then it is not a tree; but if it is a tree, it must be a true one.

Augustine: I grant that.

Reason: Now what about this: do you not grant that a tree is of that class of things that come into being and then disppear?

Augustine: I cannot deny that.

Reason: Then it must be concluded that something which is true can disappear.

Augustine: I cannot contradict that.

Reason: So does it not seem to you that truth does not disappear when true things disappear, just as chastity does not die when a chaste person dies?

Augustine: I grant that now, and eagerly await your next conclusion.

Reason: Then pay attention.

Augustine: I am.

15, 29. *Reason:* Does this statement seem true to you: "Anything which exists must exist somewhere?"

Augustine: Nothing demands my agreement more than that.

Reason: You admit that there is truth?

Augustine: I do.

Reason: Therefore we must ask where it is. For it is not in space, unless perhaps you think that something other than a body exists in space, or that truth is a body.

Augustine: I believe neither of those things.

Reason: Then where do you think it is? For if we think that it exists, it cannot be nowhere.

Augustine: If I knew where it was, perhaps I would not ask anything further.

Reason: Can you at least know where it is not?

Augustine: If you remind me, perhaps I can.

Reason: It is certainly not in mortal things. For whatever is in something cannot endure if what it is in does not endure. But it has just been granted that truth endures even when true things disappear. Therefore truth is not in mortal things. But truth exists, and cannot be nowhere. Therefore there are immortal things. But nothing is true in which there is not truth. It is settled then that there are no true things except those which are immortal. A false tree is not a tree, false wood is not wood, false silver is not silver, and anything at all which is false does not exist. But everything which is not true is false. Therefore nothing can rightly be said to exist except immortal things. Carefully go over this little bit of reasoning, to make sure there is nothing to which you cannot assent. For if it is settled, then we have nearly finished the entire task, as may become more clear in the next book.

30. *Augustine:* I thank you. I will go over these things attentively and carefully with myself and with you when we are at rest, if only that darkness does not come upon me and inflict me with its pleasures, which I dread so much.

Reason: Resolutely believe in God, and give yourself completely to him, as far as you can. Do not wish to be, as it were, your own self and under your own authority, but declare yourself the slave of the most merciful and beneficent Lord. For then he will not hesitate to raise you up to himself, and will let nothing happen to you unless it is for your own good, even though you do not know it.

Augustine: I hear, I believe, and, as far as I can, I obey; I pray to him as much as I can, so that I may do as much as I can. Or do you want anything more from me?

Reason: That's enough for now. Later, at the sight of God himself, you will do whatever he commands.

Notes

1. Augustine mentions an illness of the chest later in the *Soliloquies* (I, 14, 26) and elsewhere (*Confessions* IX, 11, 4; *Answer to the Skeptics* 1, 3; *The Happy Life* 4; Order I, 2, 5), as well as a toothache (see *Soliloquies* I, 12, 21; also *Confessions* IX, 4, 12).
2. The assertion that only the pure (of heart) can know the truth is later retracted by Augustine (*Revisions* I, 4, 2).
3. See 1 Cor 15:53-54.
4. Reading *munis*.
5. See Jn 16:13.
6. See Mt 7:13-14; Jn 14:3-7.
7. See Lk 13:24; Jn 10:7-9.
8. See Jn 16:8-11.
9. Augustine himself later corrects this phrase to "are" one (*Revisions* I, 4, 3). See Jn 10:30; 17:11.21-23.
10. Augustine here seems to be distinguishing between three definitions of "year:" 1) a year as defined by the return of the sun to its original place on the ecliptic, which thus defines the seasons by its return to the equinoxes and solstices; 2) the slightly longer period of time it takes the sun to return to its original position in reference to the fixed stars (see Ptolemy, *Almagest*, III, 1); and 3) the Great Year, when the sun and all the celestial bodies will once again be at their original positions, both in reference to the ecliptic and to the fixed stars (see Plato, *Republic*, VIII.546; *Timaeus*, 39d). This Great Year was often calculated as 36,000 years (Ptolemy, *Almagest*, VII.2, 3, following Hipparchus' data).
11. See Mt 7:8; see I, 3 above.
12. See 1 Cor 13:13; see *Soliloquies* I, 6, 12.
13. See *Order* II, 18, 47.
14. On Augustine and his (many) friends, see *Soliloquies* I, 9, 16; I, 12, 20; I, 13, 22; also *Answer to the Skeptics* II, 6, 13; *Confessions* IV, 11-18; 19, 8; *Teaching Christianity* I, 28, 29; 92; Letters 130, 13; 192, 1; 258.
15. The anima - animal wordplay in this exchange is difficult to convey in translation.
16. On Augustine's friend Alypius, see *Confessions* VI, 7-10, 11-16 and VIII, 11-12, 27-30.
17. On the (un)reliability of the senses, see *Soliloquies*, I, 24; also *Order* I, 1, 3; *Answer to the Skeptics* III, 26; *The Trinity* XV, 21; *Revisions* III, 2.
18. On Augustine's opinion of the Platonists, see *Confessions* VII, 20, 26; *Answer to the Skeptics* III, 17-20, 37-43; *The Happy Life* 1, 4.
19. On Augustine's earlier involvement with the Skeptics, see *Confessions* V, 10, 19 and V, 14, 25; *The Happy Life* 1, 4.
20. On the ship/sailing metaphor, see *The Happy Life* 1, 1-5.
21. Omitting *deo*.
22. Reading *nam mentis quasi sui sunt oculi sensus animae*.

23. See Is 6:9-10; Mt 13:10-17; Mk 4:10-12; Lk 8:9-10.
24. See 1 Cor 13:13.
25. Augustine later limits this blessedness (*Revisions* I, 4, 3).
26. On Augustine's opinion of the pursuit of wealth, see *Confessions* VI, 6, 9; *Answer to the Skeptics* I, 1, 1.
27. The book was Cicero's *Hortensius*, no longer extant; see *Confessions* III, 4, 7-8; *The Happy Life* 1, 4; *Answer to the Skeptics* I, 1, 4.
28. On Augustine's long fascination with honors and women, see *The Happy Life* 1, 4.
29. See *Confessions* VI, 11-13, 19-23.
30. See *Confessions* X, 31, 44.
31. See Cicero, *Tusculanae Disputationes* 4, 54.
32. Reading *docebo*.
33. See *Soliloquies* I, 1, 1; also *Confessions* IX, 4, 12.
34. A first century C.E. Roman encyclopedist; also mentioned by Augustine in the preface to *Heresies*.
35. A comment later regretted by Augustine (*Revisions* I, 4, 3).
36. Reading *lux sanitas*.
37. See *Revisions* I, 4, 3.
38. See *Order* I, 3.

Book II

Living, existing, understanding

1, 1. *Augustine:* Our work has been interrupted long enough; love is impatient, and there will be no end to tears, unless love is given what it loves. Therefore let us begin the second book.

Reason: Let us begin.

Augustine: Let us believe God will be near us.

Reason: Indeed, let us believe that, if it is in our power.

Augustine: God himself is our power.

Reason: Then pray as briefly and perfectly as you can.

Augustine: God, who is always the same, may I know myself, may I know you. That is my prayer.

Reason: You who wish to know yourself, do you know that you exist?

Augustine: I do.[1]

Reason: How do you know it?

Augustine: I do not know.

Reason: Do you feel yourself to be unified or differentiated?

Augustine: I do not know.

Reason: Do you know that you move?

Augustine: I do not know.

Reason: Do you know that you think?

Augustine: I do.

Reason: Therefore it is true that you think.

Augustine: That is true.

Reason: Of all these things which you say you do not know, which would you prefer to know first?

Augustine: Whether I am immortal.

Reason: You love living then?

Augustine: I admit I do.

Reason: When you have learned that you are immortal, will that be enough?

Augustine: It will indeed be a great thing, but too little for me.

Reason: How much will you rejoice over this thing which is too little?

Augustine: Very much.

Reason: Will you still cry over anything?

Augustine: Nothing at all.

Reason: What if it is found that in this life you cannot know any more than you already know, will you control your tears?

Augustine: No, I will cry so much that life will be nothing at all.

Reason: Therefore you do not love living for its own sake, but for the sake of knowing.

Augustine: I agree with that conclusion.

Reason: What if the very knowledge of these things were to make you miserable?

Augustine: I believe there is no way that could happen. But if it is so, then no one can be happy, for my ignorance of things is the only reason that I am now miserable. If knowledge of things makes one miserable, then misery is eternal.

Reason: Now I see all that you desire. Because you believe that no one is miserable on account of knowledge, from this it seems reasonable that understanding brings happiness. But no one is happy unless he or she is alive, and no one is alive who does not exist. Therefore, you want to exist, to live, and to understand; but you want to exist so that you may live, and to live so that you may understand. Therefore you know that you exist, that you live, and that you understand. But you want to know whether these will always exist, or none of them will continue to exist; whether one will always remain, while another fades away; or whether, if all remain, they can be decreased or increased.

Augustine: That is so.

Reason: Therefore, if we can prove that we will live forever, it will follow that we will exist forever.

Augustine: That will follow.

Reason: Then the question of understanding will still remain.

Truth cannot perish

2, 2. *Augustine:* I see that the order is most clear and concise.

Reason: Then be ready now to answer my questions carefully and straightforwardly.

Augustine: I am ready.

Reason: If this world will last forever, is it true that the world will last forever?

Augustine: Who would doubt that?

Reason: But if it will not last, is it not also true that the world will not last?

Augustine: I do not deny it.

Reason: Then when it disappears, if it is to disappear, will it not then be true that the world has disappeared? For as long as it is not true that the world has perished, then it has not perished. Therefore, if the world has perished, then it is not the case that it is not true that the world has perished.

Augustine: I grant that.

Reason: What about this: does it seem to you that something true can exist, while truth does not exist?

Augustine: In no way.

Reason: Therefore truth will exist, even if the world passes away.

Augustine: I cannot deny that.

Reason: And if truth itself perishes, will it not be true that truth has perished?

Augustine: Who would deny that?

Reason: But something true cannot exist, if truth does not exist.

Augustine: I granted that a little while ago.

Reason: Therefore, truth cannot possibly perish.

Augustine: Proceed as you have begun, for nothing is more true than this conclusion.

The soul lives forever

3, 3. *Reason:* Now I want you to tell me whether it seems to you that the soul or the body has sense perception.

Augustine: It seems to me that the soul does.

Reason: Does it seem to you that understanding belongs to the soul?

Augustine: So it clearly seems.

Reason: Only to the soul, or to something else?

Augustine: I see nothing other than the soul and God, in which I believe understanding could exist.

Reason: Now let us look at this. If someone were to say to you that this wall is not a wall, but a tree, what would you think?

Augustine: That either his senses or mine were deceived, or else that this is the word he uses for "wall."

Reason: But if it appeared to him as a tree and to you as a wall, could not both be true?

Augustine: In no way, for one thing cannot be both a tree and a wall. For even though to each of us it may appear to be one thing, one of us must be receiving a false impression.

Reason: What if it is neither a wall nor a tree, and both of you are mistaken?

Augustine: That is indeed possible.

Reason: Then you neglected that possibility before.

Augustine: I admit that I did.

Reason: But if the two of you admit that it seems to you other than it is, will you still both be deceived?

Augustine: No.

Reason: Therefore, that which is seen can be false, without deceiving the one who sees.

Augustine: That is possible.

Reason: Therefore we must admit that the one who sees false things is not deceived, but only the one who accepts false things.

Augustine: Clearly we must admit that.

Reason: Why then is a false thing false?

Augustine: Because it is other than it seems to be.

Reason: Therefore, if there were no one to see it, nothing would be false.

Augustine: That follows.

Reason: Therefore, deceit is not in things, but in the senses, for the one who does not accept false things is not deceived. It has been concluded that we are one thing and

the senses another, because we are able to remain unde-
ceived, even when they are deceived.

Augustine: I cannot argue with that.

Reason: But when the soul is deceived, would you dare say
that you are not deceived?

Augustine: How could I dare say that?

Reason: But there are no senses without the soul, and no
deceit without the senses. Therefore the soul either causes
deceit, or goes along with it.

Augustine: What has gone before forces my agreement.

4. *Reason:* Now answer me this: does it seem possible to
you that at some time deceit might not exist?

Augustine: How could it seem that way to me, when there
is so much difficulty in finding the truth that it would be
more ludicrous to say that deceit could not exist than to say
that truth could not exist?

Reason: Do you think that one who is not alive can have
sense perception?

Augustine: That is impossible.

Reason: Then the conclusion is that the soul lives forever.

Augustine: You are bringing me to joy too quickly; please
go more slowly.

Reason: But if these points have been rightly made, I see
no reason to doubt this.

Augustine: I still say it is too quick. I am more easily
persuaded to think that I have conceded something carelessly, than that I am now assured of the immortality of the
soul. Nevertheless, explain this conclusion and show how it
has been proven.

Reason: You said that deceit cannot exist without the
senses, and also that deceit cannot fail to exist; therefore the
senses always exist. But there are no senses without the

soul; therefore the soul is eternal. Nor can it sense, unless it is alive; therefore the soul lives forever.

The cosmic soul

4, 5. *Augustine:* What a "dagger of lead"![2] You could have concluded that humanity is immortal if I had granted that this world cannot exist without humanity, and that this world will last forever.

Reason: You really are on your guard. Nonetheless, what we have concluded is no small thing: the natural world cannot exist without the soul, unless perhaps there will be a time when there will be no deceit in nature.

Augustine: I admit that is a logical consequence. But I think that now we should more fully consider whether what has been concluded thus far is not insecure. For I see that a not insignificant step has been made toward the immortality of the soul.

Reason: Have you reflected enough on whether you may have conceded something carelessly?

Augustine: I have considered it enough, but I see nothing that would make me accuse myself of carelessness.

Reason: Therefore it is concluded that the natural world cannot exist without a living soul.

Augustine: It is so concluded, so long as it is noted that some may be born, alternating with others who die.

Reason: But if deceit were removed from the natural world, would not the result be that all things are true?

Augustine: I see how that follows.

Reason: Tell me in what way this wall seems to you to be a true wall.

Augustine: Because I am not deceived by its appearance.

Reason: That is to say, because it is just as it seems to be.

Augustine: Exactly.

Reason: If, therefore, something is false because it seems to be something other than it is, and something is true because it is as it seems, then if the one seeing were removed, nothing would be either false or true. But if deceit does not exist in the natural world, then all things are true; nor can anything be seen except by a living soul. Therefore the soul remains in the natural world, whether or not deceit can be removed.

Augustine: I see that what has been concluded thus far has been made more secure, but we have advanced no further by this addition. For the problem which bothers me the most still remains: that souls are born and then disappear, and they are always in the world not because of their immortality, but because they succeed one another.

6. *Reason:* Does it seem to you that corporeal, sensible things can be grasped by the intellect?

Augustine: It does not seem so.

Reason: Does it seem to you that God knows things by using the senses?

Augustine: I dare not say such a thing carelessly, but as far as one is allowed to speculate, God in no way uses the senses.

Reason: Therefore we conclude that only the soul can use the senses.

Augustine: For now, conclude whatever seems probable.

Reason: Do you grant that this wall, if it is not a true wall, is not a wall?

Augustine: I would grant nothing more easily.

Reason: And that something is a body only if it is a true body?

Augustine: That is so.

Reason: Therefore, if nothing is true unless it is as it seems, and something corporeal can be seen only by the senses, and only the soul can use the senses, and if something is a body only if it is a true body, then it follows that a body cannot exist unless there is a soul.

Augustine: You are pressing me too much, and I cannot offer any resistance.

Appearances

5, 7. *Reason:* Pay more careful attention to these things.

Augustine: I am with you.

Reason: This is certainly a stone, and a true one if it is not other than it seems. It is not a stone if it is not a true one. Further, it cannot be seen except by the senses.

Augustine: That is so.

Reason: Therefore, there are no stones in the deepest bowels of the earth, or anywhere else where there is no one to sense them. Even this one would not be a stone if we did not look at it, and it will not be a stone when we leave and there is no one to look at it. And if you close some boxes tightly, no matter how much you put in them, they will be empty; even the wood itself on the inside is not wood, for anything which is in the depths of a non-transparent body is hidden from all the senses, and must therefore not exist. For if it existed, it would be true; but nothing is true, unless it is as it seems. Because that is not seen, it is therefore not true. Or do you have some answer to this?

Augustine: I see that this is derived from those points which I have conceded. But it is so ludicrous that I would deny any one of them rather than concede that this is true.

Reason: I have no objection. See which you would rather say: that corporeal things can be seen only by the senses, or that only the soul can use the senses, or that a stone or something else can exist without being true, or that the true itself is to be defined differently.

Augustine: Let us examine that last one, please.

8. *Reason:* Define "true" then.

Augustine: That is true which is as it seems to the knower who wants and is able to know.

Reason: Therefore, will that which no one can know not be true? Furthermore, if that which is other than it seems is false, then if this stone seems to one person to be a stone, but to another a piece of wood, will the same thing be both false and true?

Augustine: The first possibility bothers me more. How can it be that because something cannot be known, it therefore is not true? I am not too troubled by one thing being both true and false at the same time. For I see that one thing can at the same time be both larger and smaller when compared to different things. And from this it follows that nothing is of itself larger or smaller; these words are used for comparison.

Reason: But if you say that nothing is true of itself, are you not afraid that it may follow that nothing exists of itself? For because this is wood, it is therefore true wood; and it cannot be wood of itself (that is, without a knower), unless it is true wood.

Augustine: Therefore I say this, and thus I define it; nor am I afraid that my definition may be rejected as too brief. It seems to me that the "true" is that which exists.

Reason: Therefore nothing will be false, for whatever exists is true.

Augustine: You have driven me to great distress, and I can find no reply. That is why, although I do not want to be taught in any other way than by these questions, nevertheless I fear being questioned.

Resemblance and the senses

6, 9. *Reason:* God, to whom we have committed ourselves, without a doubt gives us aid and frees us from these difficulties, if only we believe and pray most devoutly.

Augustine: Certainly there is nothing I would do more willingly at this point, for never have I been so engulfed by darkness. God, our Father, who calls upon us to pray, and who grants what you are asked for, since, when we pray, we live better and are better; listen to me, trembling in this darkness, and stretch out your right hand to me. Extend your light on to me and call me back from my wanderings, so that by your guidance I may return to myself and to you.[3] Amen.

Reason: Follow this as much as you can, and pay attention most carefully.

Augustine: Tell me, please, whatever occurs to you, so that we may not be lost.

Reason: Stay with me.

Augustine: You have my attention: I am doing nothing else.

10. *Reason:* First, we must thoroughly go over what is "the false."

Augustine: I wonder if it will be anything other than that which is not as it seems.

Reason: Pay attention rather, and let us first ask the senses themselves. For certainly that which the eyes see is not called false unless it bears some resemblance to the true. For example, a man whom we see in our dreams is not a true man, but a false one, precisely because he bears a resemblance to the true. For who would see a dog in a dream and rightly say that he dreamed of a man? Therefore, that dog is false because it resembles a true one.

Augustine: It is as you say.

Reason: What if someone who is awake were to see a horse and think that he sees a man: would he not be deceived precisely because something resembling a man appeared to him? For if nothing other than the image of a horse appeared to him, he could not think that he sees a man.

Augustine: I agree completely.

Reason: We also speak of a false tree which we see in a picture, a false face which is reflected in a mirror, the false motion of towers as seen by those sailing by, a false break in an oar in the water:[4] these are false for no other reason than that they resemble the true.

Augustine: I grant that.

Reason: We are deceived in the same way regarding twins, eggs, the seals made by one signet ring, and other things of this kind.

Augustine: I follow you completely and grant that.

Reason: Therefore the resemblance of things which relates to the eyes is the mother of deception.

Augustine: I cannot disagree.

11. *Reason:* Unless I am mistaken, all this data can be divided into two types: one is concerned with equal things, the other with inferior things. They are equal when we say that this resembles that and that resembles this, as is said of twins or the impressions of a signet ring. But when we speak of inferior things, we say only that the inferior thing resembles the superior thing. For who would look in a mirror and

rightly say that he or she resembles the image, rather than that it resembles him or her? That which the soul experiences, together with the things which are seen, makes up this type. But the soul experiences something either in the sense itself, such as the non-existent motion of the tower; or within itself, such as the visions of dreamers and perhaps also of the insane. Furthermore, those resemblances which appear in the things which we see are composed and formed, some by nature, others by living things. Nature makes inferior resemblances either by producing them or reflecting them: by producing them, as when children are born who resemble their parents; by reflecting them, as in any kind of mirror. (Even though people make the majority of mirrors, they nevertheless do not fashion the images which are reflected in them.) The works of living things are in pictures and any other creation of this kind; those made by demons (if they exist) can be included in this category.[5] But as for the shadows of bodies, they are quite rightly said to resemble bodies and to be like false bodies; therefore, they must be said to belong to the judgment of the eyes, and should be put in that category of resemblances which nature makes by reflection. For every body exposed to light reflects it, and casts a shadow on the opposite side. Does any of this seem objectionable to you?

Augustine: Nothing at all. But I am eager to see where this is going.

12. *Reason:* We must be patient until the other senses tell us that deception resides in the resemblance to the true. For in hearing almost as many types of resemblances occur, as when we hear the voice of someone speaking, but do not see him or her, we think it is someone else whose voice is similar. Or in inferior resemblances, an echo is a good example, or a ringing in the ears, or the imitation by clocks

of a blackbird or raven, or the sounds dreaming or insane people think they hear. And falsetto voices, as they are called by musicians, bear witness in an astonishing way to this truth, as will be shown later; it is enough for now to note that they do not lack a resemblance to true voices. Do you follow this?

Augustine: With the greatest pleasure. I have no difficulty in understanding it.

Reason: Then let us not delay. Does it seem possible to you that one could distinguish one lily from another just by smell, or the honey from different hives just by taste, or the softness of swan feathers from that of goose feathers just by touch?

Augustine: It does not seem so to me.

Reason: Then when we dream of such smells or tastes or touches, are we not deceived by the resemblance of the image; and the imperfection of the resemblance increases as it is more unreal?

Augustine: What you say is true.

Reason: Therefore it is clear that in all our senses we are deceived by an enticing resemblance, whether it is between equal things or inferior things. Even if we are not deceived, because we keep ourselves from agreeing or because we see the difference, nevertheless we call things false because we see in them a resemblance to the true.

Augustine: I cannot doubt that.

Similarity and dissimilarity; Soliloquies

7, 13. *Reason:* Now pay attention while we go back over these things, so that what we are trying to show may become clearer.

Augustine: I am here; say what you wish. I have decided once for all to last through this indirect course and not drop out, so great is my hope of attaining the goal for which I feel we are striving.

Reason: Well done. Now consider whether it seems to you that when we see similar eggs we can rightly say that any one of them is false.

Augustine: It does not seem so at all. For if they are eggs, then they are all true eggs.

Reason: When we see an image reflected in a mirror, what indications cause us to perceive that it is false?

Augustine: Because it cannot be grasped, it makes no sound, it does not move of itself, it is not alive, and so many others that it would take too long to list them.

Reason: I see that you do not want to delay and your haste must be obliged. So as not to repeat each example, if those people whom we see in dreams were able to live, speak, and be touched by those who are awake, and if there were no difference between them and those whom we see and speak to when we are awake and clear-headed, would we say they are false?

Augustine: How could one rightly say that?

Reason: Therefore, if they are true because they most closely resemble the true and there is no difference at all between them and the true ones, and if they would be false, if they were shown to be dissimilar because of differences of some kind or another, then must it not be concluded that similarity is the mother of truth and dissimilarity the mother of deception?

Augustine: I can say nothing, and I am ashamed at my earlier careless agreement.

14. *Reason:* It is absurd for you to be ashamed; it is for this very reason that we chose this type of discourse. Because we

are talking with ourselves alone, I want to entitle it *Solilo-quies*.[6] This name may be new and perhaps unrefined, but quite appropriate for explaining the work. There is no better way to seek the truth than by question and answer, but hardly anyone can be found who would not be ashamed at being proven wrong in an argument. This almost always results in a topic for discussion which has started well, being drowned out by the unruly clamor of obstinacy, along with hurt feelings which are usually hidden, but sometimes are out in the open. For these reasons, it seemed to me that the most peaceful and proper way to seek the truth with God's help would be by questioning and answering myself. So there is nothing to fear: if you have carelessly entangled yourself at any point, go back and free yourself, for otherwise one cannot escape.

Turmoils with Reason

8, 15. *Augustine:* What you say is right. But I cannot see clearly what I have wrongly agreed to, unless perhaps it was when I stated that the false is rightly said to be that which bears a resemblance to the true; but nothing else occurs to me as deserving of the name of false. Nevertheless, I am forced to admit that the things called false are so called because they differ from the true, and from this it is concluded that dissimilarity itself is the cause of deception. So I am in distress, for I cannot easily conceive of something which is produced by opposite causes.

Reason: What if this is the only case of its kind in the natural world? You are aware, are you not, that if you were to examine the innumerable species of animals, you would find that only the crocodile moves its upper jaw when chewing? Besides, one can scarcely find something that is so similar to another that it is not also dissimilar in some way.

Augustine: I see that. But when I consider that what we call false has both something similar and something dissimilar to the true, I cannot decide for which of these it deserves the name of false. For if I say that it is because it is dissimilar, then there will be nothing which cannot be called false, for there is nothing which is not dissimilar to something which we accept as true. But if I say that it should be called false because it is similar, then not only will those eggs object (for they are true precisely because they are so similar), but I will also not be able to resist anyone who will force me to admit that everything is false, since I cannot deny that all things are similar in some way. But suppose I were not afraid to say that both similarity and dissimilarity at the same time cause something to be rightly called false. Will you give me some way of escape then? For I will still be compelled to declare that everything is false, since, as we said earlier, all things are found to be partly similar and partly dissimilar. Nothing would be left for me, except to say that the false is that which is other than it seems; but that would terrify me with all those monsters, past which I thought I had already sailed. I am again driven back by an unexpected whirlwind, so that I call true that which is as it seems. It follows from this that nothing can be true without someone to know it, and this is for me a terrible shipwreck on hidden rocks (which are true even if they are unknown). And if I say that the true is that which exists, then it will follow that the false does not exist anywhere, which anyone would deny. And so these turmoils return, and I see no progress, in spite of my patience with your delays.

A definition of false

9, 16. *Reason:* Pay attention rather, for I will never admit that we have begged for divine help in vain. I see that, having investigated everything as best we can, there is nothing left that can rightly by called false, unless it would be that which either presents itself as something it is not, or tries to exist entirely and fails. But the first type of falsehood is either deceptive or untrue. That is rightly called deceptive which includes the desire to deceive; that is inconceivable without a soul, though it is partly from reason, partly from nature. It is from reason in rational animals, such as human beings; from nature in beasts, such as the fox. But the other kind, which I call untrue, is found in those who lie. They differ from those who are deceptive, in that everyone who is deceptive wishes to deceive, but not everyone who lies wishes to deceive. For masques and comedies and many poems are full of lies, but their purpose is to delight rather than to deceive; and nearly everyone who tells a joke is telling a lie. But one is rightly called deceptive or deceiving, if his or her goal is to deceive someone. Those who do it not in order to deceive, but just make something up, no one hesitates to call liars, or if not that, at least tellers of lies. Or do you have anything to say against this?

17. *Augustine:* Please proceed. Perhaps now you have begun to teach me some un-false things about the false. But now I am waiting to hear about that class which you spoke of, the kind that tries to be and fails.

Reason: Why would not you wait? Those are the things we have discussed so much already. Does it not seem to you that your image in a mirror wants, in a way, to be you, and is false because it is not?

Augustine: That certainly seems so.

Reason: Do not all pictures and replicas of that kind and all artists' works of that type strive to be that in whose likeness they are made?

Augustine: I am completely convinced that they do.

Reason: And I think you would agree that those things which deceive people who are asleep or insane are of that class.

Augustine: Those more than others. For those try more than others to be the things which people who are awake and sane perceive, and they are false because they cannot be what they try to be.

Reason: Then should I say more about the motion of towers or the oar in the water or the shadows of bodies? I think it is clear that they are to be measured by this rule.

Augustine: That is most clear.

Reason: I will pass over the other senses, for anyone who considers this will find that, among the things we perceive by sense, a thing is called false if it tries to be something and fails.

Contradictory elements

10, 18. *Augustine:* What you say is correct. But I am surprised that you exclude from this category those poems and jokes and other falsehoods.

Reason: Because it is one thing to want to be false, and another to be unable to be true. Therefore we cannot[7] put human works such as comedies, tragedies, masques, and other things of that type in the same category as the works of painters and other image-makers. For a picture of a man cannot be as true, even though it tries to look like a man, as those things which are written in the books of the comic authors. Those things do not wish to be false, nor are they false because they try to be so, but by necessity they conform as much as possible to the artist's design. But on the stage Roscius was a false Hecuba by his own will, though by nature a true man; he was by his own will a true tragic actor, because he played his part, but a false Priam, because he imitated Priam though he was not Priam.[8] From this there arises something remarkable, but something which no one would deny.

Augustine: What is that?

Reason: What do you think? It is that these things are in some way true precisely because they are in some way false, and their being true is supported only by their being false in another way. So they cannot possibly be what they want or ought to be if they avoid being false. For how could that man I just mentioned be a true tragic actor if he were unwilling to be a false Hector, a false Andromache, a false Hercules, and any number of others? Or how could the picture be true, if the horse were not false? How could the image of the man in the mirror be true, if the man were not false? Then if some things are helped to be true by their being something false, why do we so greatly fear falsehoods and strive for truth as for some great good?

Augustine: I do not know. I would be greatly surprised by this, if it were not for the fact that I see nothing in these examples worthy of imitation. Unlike actors or reflections in a mirror or the bronze cows of Myron,[9] we need not adapt or accommodate ourselves to the character of another; we need not become false in order to be true to our own character. We should seek that which is true, rather than something with two contradictory faces, true on the one side, false on the other.

Reason: You require great and divine things. If we find such things, will we not admit that these things produce and in a way form truth itself, from which everything which is in any way called true gets its name?

Augustine: I willingly agree.

The discipline of grammar

11, 19. *Reason:* Does the discipline of disputation seem to you true or false?

Augustine: Who would doubt that it is true? But grammar is also true.

Reason: Just as true?

Augustine: I do not see how anything could be more true than the true.

Reason: What about that which has nothing false in it? When considering this a little while ago, you were annoyed by those things which in some unknown way could not be true unless they were false. Or are you unaware that all those fables and obvious falsehoods are related to grammar?

Augustine: I am aware of that. But I do not think they are false because of grammar; rather, grammar shows them for what they are. A fable is a lie made up for either profit or pleasure. Grammar is the discipline which preserves and governs the spoken word. Because of its place, it must gather all the works of human language, even fictions, which have been committed to memory or writing. It does not create falsehoods, but from them it teaches and presents a true system.[10]

Reason: Well said. Right now I do not care whether you define and distinguish these things well: I want to ask whether grammar itself or the discipline of disputation shows that this is so.

Augustine: I do not deny that the capability and skill of defining by which I tried to divide these things are a part of the art of disputation.

20. *Reason:* What about grammar itself? If it is true, is it not true precisely because it is a discipline? It is called "discipline" because it comes from "learning."[11] No one who has learned something and held on to it can be said not to know, and no one knows false things. Therefore every discipline is true.

Augustine: I see nothing that has been carelessly agreed to in this little bit of reasoning. Nevertheless, I am worried that it might seem to someone that therefore those fables are also true, because we learn them and hold on to them.

Reason: Did our teacher not want us to believe and to know the things which he taught?

Augustine: Oh yes, he insisted very forcefully that we know them.

Reason: Did he ever insist that we believe that Daedalus had flown?

Augustine: He never did that. But he certainly made sure that if we did not hold on to the fable in our minds, then we could hardly hold on to anything with our hands.[12]

Reason: Then do you deny that it is true that this is a fable and that this is how Daedalus has become famous?

Augustine: I do not deny that is true.

Reason: Then you do not deny that you learned something true when you learned these things. For if it were true that Daedalus had flown, but children learned and recited it as a made-up story, then they would be holding on to a false notion, because what they were reciting really was true. So the thing we were surprised at before has come up again:

there could be no true fable about the flight of Daedalus, unless it were false that Daedalus had flown.

Augustine: I grasp that. But I'm waiting to see how that will help us.

Reason: Is it not clear now that the reasoning is not false, by which we concluded that a discipline cannot be a discipline unless it teaches true things?

Augustine: And how does that relate?

Reason: Because I want you to tell me how grammar is a discipline, since it is true because it is a discipline.

Augustine: I do not know how I should respond.

Reason: Does it not seem to you that it could not possibly be a discipline if nothing were defined in it, and if it had no divisions and distinctions into classes and types?

Augustine: Now I see what you are saying. No kind of discipline occurs to me in which there are no definitions and divisions and reasoning to determine what something really is, assigning to each thing what belongs to it, without any confusion of the parts,[13] omitting nothing intrinsic to it, and including nothing extrinsic; all of this together makes what is called a discipline.

Reason: Therefore, on account of all that, it is called true.

Augustine: I see how that follows.

21. *Reason:* Now tell me which discipline contains the principles of definition, division, and distribution?

Augustine: It has already been said that these are contained in the rules of disputation.

Reason: Therefore grammar, as a discipline and as something true, comes from that art which you said before is free from deception. And it seems to me that one may conclude this not only of grammar, but of all disciplines. For you said, and said truly, that no discipline occurred to you in which the ability of defining and dividing was not what made it a discipline. But if they are true for the same reason that they are disciplines, will anyone deny that all disciplines are true through truth itself?

Augustine: I agree almost completely. But it bothers me that we count the system of disputation among these disciplines. So I think rather that truth is that through which this system is true.

Reason: Very good; you are really wide awake. But I do not think that you would deny that disputation is true for the same reason that it is a discipline.

Augustine: Indeed, that is what bothers me. For as I noted, it is itself a discipline, and for that reason it is called true.

Reason: But do you think that it could be a discipline, unless everything in it were defined and divided?

Augustine: I could say nothing other than that.

Reason: So if this requirement is governed by disputation, then that discipline is true because of itself. Who will think it remarkable if that through which all things are true is of itself and in itself the true truth?

Augustine: There is nothing to keep me from going along with this opinion.

The subject and what is in the subject

12, 22. *Reason:* Then pay attention to what little remains.

Augustine: Show me whatever you have; as long as it is something I can understand, I will readily agree to it.

Reason: It has not escaped our notice that something is said to be in something else in two ways. The first way is such that the thing can be separated and exist somewhere else: for example, wood in this place, or the sun in the east. The second way is such that the thing is in a subject and cannot be separated from it: for example, the form and appearance which we see in this wood, or light in the sun, or heat in fire, or a discipline in the soul, or other similar things. Does it seem otherwise to you?

Augustine: We are well acquainted with these: most eagerly we learned and knew them from early childhood. So if I am asked about them I can only agree without any hesitation.

Reason: Then do you not agree that whatever is inseparably in a subject cannot endure if the subject itself does not endure?

Augustine: I see how that follows. For anyone who considers the matter closely understands that even when the subject endures, what is in the subject may not endure. The color of one's body can change, either because of health or age, even though the body itself has not perished. This is not true in all cases, but only in those in which the things exist in the subjects, but are not necessary to the subjects' existence. For a wall to exist it need not have the color we see in it, since it would still be a wall and be called such, even if it were to turn black or white or some other color. On the other hand, a fire without heat would not be a fire, and we cannot call something snow unless it is white.

The immortality of the soul

13, 23. But as for your question, would anyone agree or even think it possible that something which is in a subject endures when the subject itself has perished? It is bizarre and far from the truth to think that something which could not exist unless it were in something else could still exist when that something has disappeared.

Reason: Then what we were looking for has been found.

Augustine: What are you talking about?

Reason: Just what you hear.

Augustine: Then it is clearly established that the soul is immortal?

Reason: If the things you have agreed to are true, then it is most clear; unless perhaps you say that even when the soul dies it is still the soul.

Augustine: I would never say that, but I do say that because it perishes, the soul therefore ceases to exist. And I will not withdraw this statement because great philosophers have said that the thing which brings life wherever it goes cannot receive death into itself. For even though light illuminates wherever it can enter and cannot receive darkness into itself (because of that notable law about opposites), nevertheless it is extinguished and the place is darkened when the light is put out. So that which held back the darkness and would never receive it into itself nevertheless gave way to the darkness by dying, just as it could have done by leaving. So I fear that death may come upon the body as darkness comes to a place, sometimes by the soul leaving, sometimes by its being extinguished, just as with light. Therefore there can be no confidence about all types of bodily death, although some kind of death should be wished for, one in which the soul is safely led from the body and brought to a place (if there is such a place) where it cannot be extinguished. But if this is impossible and the soul is in the body like a burning lamp, and cannot endure outside of it, and every death is the extinction of soul or life in the body, then some kind of life should be chosen (insofar as one is allowed) in which one lives one's life in confidence and tranquility. But I do not know how this is possible if the soul dies. How happy are those who are persuaded, either by themselves or someone else, that death is not to be feared, even if the soul perishes!

But as for pitiful me, no reasoning and no books have been able to convince me.

24. *Reason:* Stop your moaning. The human soul is immortal.

Augustine: How do you prove it?

Reason: From those things which I think you have already agreed to very cautiously.

Augustine: I do not recall giving any careless answers to your questions. But please sum it all up now. Let us see how far we have come after so many digressions, though I do not want you to question me any more. For if you briefly list those things to which I have agreed, then why would you want me to answer them again? Are you arbitrarily putting obstacles in the way of my joy, if perhaps we have accomplished some good?

Reason: I will do what you seem to wish, but pay attention most carefully.

Augustine: Tell me and I will pay attention. Why do you torment me?

Reason: If everything which is in a subject endures forever, then the subject itself must necessarily endure forever. Every discipline is in the soul as in a subject. Therefore, if the discipline endures forever, then necessarily the soul endures forever. But a discipline is the truth, and the truth endures forever, as reason showed at the beginning of this book. Hence the soul endures forever, and the soul cannot be said to die.[14] Therefore the only one who can deny the soul's immortality without being absurd would be someone who can show that something in the preceding argument has been concluded incorrectly.

Various quandaries

14, 25. *Augustine:* Now I wish to let myself rejoice, but I hold myself back somewhat for two reasons. The first thing that bothers me is that we have used such a convoluted path, following some unknown line of reasoning, when everything that is at issue could have been demonstrated briefly, as now it has been. So it makes me uneasy that the conversation has wandered about in a way that almost seems treacherous. Secondly, I do not see how a discipline, especially that of disputation, always exists in the soul, when so few are aware of it, and even someone who now knows it knew nothing of it for a long time, starting at infancy. For we cannot say that the souls of the uneducated are not souls, or that there is in the soul a discipline about which they are ignorant. But if this is completely ridiculous, then it is still the case that either truth is not always in the soul, or else that discipline is not the truth.

26. *Reason:* You see that it was not for nothing that our reasoning took such devious paths. For we were inquiring about what truth is, and I see that even now we have not been able to hunt it down in this thicket of things, even though we have wandered down almost every path. But what shall we do? Are we to stop what we have begun and wait until something from someone else's book falls into our hands and answers the question sufficiently? For I think that before our time many books have been written which we have not read; and even now (and this is not just conjecture about things we are ignorant of) works in both prose and poetry have been written on this subject. These have been written by men whose works cannot remain hidden from us, and we know their skill is such that we cannot fail to find what we want in their writings. This is

especially true of that man whom we see before our eyes bringing back to life that eloquence which we grieved for as dead.[15] Will the one who taught us how to live let us be ignorant of the nature of life?

Augustine: I do not think so, and I hope for much from him. But one thing saddens me: that we cannot show him, as much as we would like to, our reverence for him and for wisdom. For certainly he would take pity on our thirst and pour out more abundantly than he does now. He is without a care, because he is already completely convinced of the soul's immortality, and does not know that there are perhaps some who know the misery of such ignorance well enough, and whom it would be cruel not to help, especially if they ask for it. There is another who knows our longing because of our close friendship,[16] but he is so far away and in our present circumstances we can hardly even send him a letter. I believe that in his leisure on the other side of the Alps he has now finished a poem in which the spellbinding fear of death is driven out, and the soul's coldness and indolence, hardened like old frost, are expelled. But meanwhile, until these things which we cannot control come about, is it not most disgraceful to waste our time and let our very soul hang in suspense for an uncertain verdict?

True and false natures

15, 27. Where are the things which we asked and go on asking God for: not riches, not bodily pleasure, not popular distinctions and honors, but only that he show us the way in our search for our soul and for him? Has he really abandoned us or been abandoned by us?

Reason: It is completely contrary to God's nature to abandon those who desire such things, and so it should be contrary to our nature to abandon such a leader. So if you please, let us retrace how we came to these two conclusions, namely, that truth endures forever and that the science of disputation is truth. For you said that these were uncertain, and therefore the whole argument would not put us at ease. Or should we rather ask how a discipline can exist in an uneducated soul, which we cannot say is not a soul? For that seemed to upset you, so that it was necessary to question again the things to which you had agreed.

Augustine: Let us discuss these first two points, and then we will look at the other. I think that in that way, no doubt will remain.

Reason: Let us do that, but give me your complete and most careful attention. For I know what happens to you when you concentrate: you focus too much on the conclusion, expecting to get to it immediately, and so you agree to questions without careful consideration.

Augustine: Perhaps what you say is true, but I will fight against this type of illness as much as I can. Begin questioning right away, so that we do not dwell on unimportant things.

28. *Reason:* As I recall, we concluded that truth cannot perish because not only if the whole world perished, but even if truth itself perished, it would still be true that the world and truth had perished. But nothing is true without truth. Therefore there is no way for truth to perish.

Augustine: I acknowledge these things and will be very astonished if they are false.

Reason: Then let us inspect the other point.

Augustine: Please let me consider this a little more, and spare me the embarrassment of going back over these things again.

Reason: Will it not be true that truth has perished? If it will not be true, then truth will not have perished. And if it will be true, how will it be true after the destruction of truth, when truth no longer exists?

Augustine: There is nothing more for me to reflect on or consider; proceed with the other point. We will certainly do what we can to make sure that learned and wise men read this and correct our carelessness, if there is any. But I do not think that I can now or at any other time find anything to object to in this.

29. *Reason:* Then is anything called truth, except that by which any true thing is true?

Augustine: Nothing at all.

Reason: Then is anything rightly called true, except that which is not false?

Augustine: To doubt that would really be insane.

Reason: Is not the false that which is like something enough to resemble it, but nevertheless is not that which it seems to resemble?

Augustine: I see nothing else which I would more readily call false. Nevertheless, one often calls false that which is far from a resemblance to the true.

Reason: Who would deny that? But it must have some similarity to the true.

Augustine: How? For when it is said that Medea flew on winged snakes tied together, this in no way imitates the true, since it is non-existent, and a thing which is completely non-existent cannot imitate anything.

Reason: What you say is correct. But you neglect the fact that something which is completely non-existent cannot be called false. For if it is false, it exists; if it does not exist, it is not false.

Augustine: Then we cannot call that outrageous story about Medea false?

Reason: No, for if it is false, how is it outrageous?

Augustine: I see this as quite astonishing. So when I hear, ". . . huge winged snakes tied to a chariot,"[17] I am not to call it false?

Reason: Certainly you do say that, for there is something in it which you call false.

Augustine: What, I ask you?

Reason: The idea which is expressed in that verse itself.

Augustine: And how does that have a similarity to the true?

Reason: Because it would be expressed in a similar way even if Medea had truly done that. Therefore a false idea imitates true ideas by its expression itself. If it is not believed, then it imitates true ideas only in the way it is said, so it is only false and not deceptive. But if it gains credibility, then it imitates true ideas which are believed.

Augustine: Now I understand that there is a great difference between what we say and the things about which we speak. Now I agree (for only this held me back) that we do not rightly call something false unless it has a similarity to something true. Who would not be justly laughed at if he said that a stone is false silver? But if someone were to say that a stone is silver, we would say that he has said something false, that is, that he presents a false idea. But I do not think that it is ridiculous to call tin or lead false silver, because the thing itself imitates silver; in this instance, it is not our idea which is false, but the thing of which we speak.

16, 30. *Reason:* You understand it well. But consider whether we can properly call silver by the name of false lead.

Augustine: I would not call it that.

Reason: Why not?

Augustine: I do not know; but I see that it is very much against my inclination to say that.

Reason: Is it perhaps because silver is finer, and it would be a sort of insult to call it that, while it is something of an honor for lead to be called false silver?

Augustine: You have explained it exactly as I wished. For the same reason I believe that men who wear women's clothes are justly deemed disgraceful and dishonorable. I do not know if I should call them false women or false men. Nevertheless, we can without hesitation call them true actors and truly disgraceful. If they stay hidden, I think we can call them, not without truth, truly base, since one is called disgraceful only when widely known as evil.

Reason: There will be another occasion for us to discuss these things, for there are many things which seem to most people to have a shameful appearance, but nevertheless are shown to be honorable because of their praiseworthy goal. It is a tough question, whether one, in order to free his homeland, ought to deceive the enemy by putting on women's clothing; perhaps he would become a truer man by being a false woman. Or should a wise man, who is certain that in some way his life is necessary for humanity, prefer to die of cold rather than put on feminine clothes, when there is nothing else to wear? But, as I said, we will see about this some other time. Clearly you can tell how much inquiry is necessary in order to determine how far these things can be taken without becoming inexcusable disgraces. Now it is enough for the present question, I think, that it is clear and cannot be doubted that nothing is false except by some similarity to the true.

Truth is neither body nor emptiness

17, 31. *Augustine:* Go on to the remaining questions, for I am thoroughly convinced of this.

Reason: Then I want to ask this: besides the disciplines in which we are trained and among which the study of wisdom should be counted, can we find anything which is so true that it is not false in one way so that it can be true in another, like an Achilles in a play?

Augustine: It seems to me that many could be found. For the disciplines do not contain this stone; nor does it, in order to be a true stone, imitate something else, next to which it would be called false. And from this one observation you can see the innumerable others which must be omitted, but which immediately occur to any thinking person.

Reason: I certainly see that. But do they not all seem to you to be included under the one title of body?

Augustine: They would seem so, if I were certain that emptiness is nothing,[18] or if I thought that the soul itself is counted among corporeal things, or if I believed that God is a body of some kind. If all these things exist, I do not see that they are either false or true by their imitation of something else.

Reason: You are sending us on a long trip, but I will take a short-cut as much as I can. For certainly what you call emptiness is quite different from what you call truth.

Augustine: Very different. For what would be more empty than myself if I thought that truth is something empty, or if

I so eagerly sought something empty? What else other than truth do I long to find?

Reason: Then perhaps you agree that nothing is true which is not made true by the truth.

Augustine: That has been clear for some time now.

Reason: Do you doubt that nothing is empty except emptiness itself, or at least that a body is not empty?

Augustine: I do not doubt that at all.

Reason: Then I suppose you believe that truth is some kind of body.

Augustine: Not at all.

Reason: Maybe it is in a body?

Augustine: I do not know. But it is not to the point, for I think that you know that if there is emptiness, there is more of it where there is no body.

Reason: That is certainly clear.

Augustine: Then why do we delay?

Reason: Does it seem to you that truth created emptiness, or that there can be something true where there is no truth?

Augustine: It does not seem so.

Reason: Therefore emptiness is not true, because it cannot be made by that which is not empty. Further, that which lacks truth is clearly not true, and certainly that which is called empty is called that because it is nothing. So how can that which does not exist be true, or how can that which is essentially nothing exist at all?

Augustine: Let us go on, and leave emptiness as it is — empty.

Shapes

18, 32. *Reason:* What do you say about the others?

Augustine: What others?

Reason: That which you see me affirming so much. What remains is the soul and God. If these two are true because truth is in them, then no one should doubt God's immortality. The soul is also believed to be immortal if truth, which cannot disappear, is shown to be in it also. Now let us examine this last point, whether a body is not truly true; that is, that truth is not in it, but rather a sort of image of truth. For if we find in the body, which is quite certainly subject to death, a thing which is true in the same way as something is true in the disciplines, then the discipline of disputation will no longer be the truth by which all disciplines are true. For a body is something true which does not seem to be formed by the science of disputation. But if a body is true because of some imitation, and therefore not absolutely true, then perhaps there will be nothing to keep one from saying that the science of disputation is truth itself.

Augustine: In the meantime, let us ask about the body, for I see that even when this point is settled, the argument still would not be over.

Reason: How do you know what God wants? Pay attention. I think that a body is sustained in a certain form and appearance. If it did not have this, it would not be a body, and if it had a true form and appearance, it would be a soul. Or should one think otherwise?

Augustine: I agree in part, but about the rest I am doubtful. I agree that a body cannot exist unless it has a certain shape, but I do not quite understand how it would be a soul if it had a true shape.

Reason: Do you remember nothing from the beginning of the first book and your geometry?

Augustine: It is good you reminded me. I certainly do remember, and most pleasantly at that.

Reason: Are the sorts of shapes found in bodies like those which that discipline describes?[19]

Augustine: No, it is incredible how inferior they are shown to be.

Reason: Then which of these do you think is true?

Augustine: Please do not think that I even have to be asked this. Who is so intellectually blind that he or she would not see that those shapes which are taught in geometry inhabit truth itself or truth inhabits them, while the shapes of a body, because they seem to strive in some way toward those of geometry, have some similarity to the truth and are therefore false. Now I understand everything you were trying to show me.

Immortal truth to the immortality of the soul

19, 33. *Reason:* Then why should we now inquire about the discipline of disputation? For whether the geometric shapes are in truth or truth is in them, no one doubts that they are contained in our soul, that is, in our intellect, and because of this, truth is also in our soul. But if any discipline is in the soul as if inseparably in a subject, and if truth cannot perish, then why, I ask, why do we doubt the eternal life of the soul because of some knowledge we have of death? Does the line or the square or the circle have other things which it imitates in order to be true?

Augustine: There is no way I can believe that, unless perhaps a line is something other than length without breadth, or a circle something other than a line extended around and equidistant at all points from a center.

Reason: Why then do we delay? Is the truth not where these things are?

Augustine: May God keep such madness from us.

Reason: Then is a discipline not in the soul?

Augustine: Who would say that?

Reason: But perhaps something which is in a subject can endure when the subject perishes?

Augustine: How could I be convinced of that?

Reason: Then the only possibility left is that truth disappears.

Augustine: How can that be?

Reason: Then the soul is immortal. Now believe your reasoning, believe the truth. It cries out that it lives in you, that it is immortal, and that its home cannot be taken from it by any death of the body. Turn away from your shadow, turn back toward yourself. There is no perishing in you, unless you forget that you cannot perish.

Augustine: I hear, I regain my senses, I begin to recall. But please resolve the remaining points, as to how a discipline and truth are understood to exist in an uneducated soul, if we cannot say that it is mortal.

Reason: That question requires another book, if you wish to treat it thoroughly. I also see that the questions which we have explored as best we can should be reexamined by you. If none of the things agreed to is doubtful, then I think we have attained a great deal and can ask about the other questions with no small degree of confidence.

Imagination and truth

20, 34. *Augustine:* It is just as you say, and I submit to your instructions with pleasure. But let me ask one thing before you bring this book to a close. Briefly explain the difference between a true shape which is contained in the intellect, and the kind which contemplation makes for itself and which is called in Greek phantasia or phantasm.

Reason: What you seek is something which only the purest can see, and you are poorly trained for the sight of such a thing. We have gone through these wanderings for no other reason than for your training, so that you might be fit to see it. But perhaps I can briefly make it clear to you how it can be shown that there is a great difference. Suppose that you have forgotten something, and others want to recover it in some way for your memory. Therefore they say, "Is it this or that?" citing different things as though they were similar to it. You do not see what you wish to remember, but you do see that it is not among the things mentioned to you. When this happens, does it seem to you that that memory has been completely obliterated? For that discernment which keeps you from accepting the false reminders is itself a part of remembering.

Augustine: So it seems.

Reason: Such people do not yet see the true thing, but nonetheless cannot be misled or deceived, and they know what they are seeking well enough. But if someone were to say to you that you laughed a few days after you were born, you would not dare say that it is false; and if the one who said that were someone you trusted, you would not remember it, but you would believe it, because that entire time is hidden from you in the deepest oblivion. Or do you think otherwise?

Augustine: I agree completely.

Reason: Therefore this kind differs greatly from the other kind of forgetting, which is really in the middle. For there is another kind which is more similar and nearer to remembering and receiving the truth. An example of this is when we see something, think for certain that we have seen it before, and even say that we know it, but as for where or when or how or in whose presence it came to our notice, we are hard pressed to recollect and remember. For example, if this happens to us with a person, we ask him where we met him; and when he tells us, suddenly the whole event floods back into our memory like a light and it is no longer a chore for us to remember. Is this kind of thing unknown to you or difficult to understand?

Augustine: What could be clearer, or happen to me more often?

35. *Reason:* Those who are well educated in the liberal arts are like this. While learning, they uncover and in some way dig up things which were undoubtedly buried in forgetfulness.[20] Nevertheless, they are not satisfied and will not stop until they gaze fully and completely at the face of truth, whose splendor shines faintly in those arts. But from these arts some false colors and forms pour, as it were, into the mirror of thought, and often mislead those who make inquiries, and deceive those who think that what they know or inquire about is all there is. Such imaginations are to be avoided with great caution. Their deceit is detected when they change with what we called the changing mirror of thought, while the face of truth remains single and invariable. For example, thought depicts to itself squares of varying sizes and, so to speak, holds them before the eyes. But the inner mind, which wishes to see what is true, turns rather, if it can, toward that according to which it judges that all these are squares.

Augustine: What if someone says to us that the mind judges according to what it is used to seeing with the eyes?

Reason: If it is so taught, then why does it judge that a true sphere, of whatever size, is touched by a true plane at only one point? Does the eye see, or can it see such a thing, when something of this kind cannot be formed even by the imagination of thought? And do we not prove this when we represent with the mind's imagination the smallest circle imaginable, and then draw lines from it to its center? For when we draw two lines, between which one could hardly stick a needle, we cannot, even in our imagination, draw other lines between them, such that they would reach the center without touching each other. But reason declares that innumerable lines can be drawn, even in these unbelievably narrow spaces, which can touch only in the center, and that a circle could be drawn in every intervening space. Since imagination — phantasia — cannot do this and is even inferior to the eyes themselves (for through them this imagination intrudes upon the mind), it is clear that it differs greatly from the truth, which cannot be seen as long as this image is seen.

36. These things will be discussed with more care and precision when we begin to examine the understanding, which is the next part of our exposition.[21] There we will explain and discuss, as best we can, any concerns about the life of the soul. For I believe that you have more than a little fear that human death, although it may not destroy the soul, may nonetheless bring forgetfulness of everything and of truth itself, if any truth has been gathered.

Augustine: One cannot assert enough how fearful that evil is. For what would eternal life be like, or what death would not be preferable to it, if the soul only lives as we see it living in a newly born infant (to say nothing of the life that is in the womb, for I think that it also exists there)?

Reason: Be of good spirit. We know God will help us in our search. God promises that after this body we will have the greatest blessing and the greatest fullness of truth, without any deception.

Augustine: May what we hope for come to pass.

Notes

1. On the minimal amount of certain knowledge available to us, see *The Happy Life* 7; *Answer to the Skeptics* III, 9, 18-19; *Free Will* I, 7, 16 and II, 3, 7; *The Trinity* XV, 11, 21; *Teaching Christianity* IV, 11, 26.
2. A quotation from Cicero, *De finibus bonorum et malorum* 4, 48.
3. See *Soliloquies* II, 19, 33; also *Confessions* VII, 10, 16; *Answer to the Skeptics* I, 8, 23 and II, 2, 5; *Order* I, 1, 3.
4. The same examples are used by Augustine in *Answer to the Skeptics* III, 11, 26.
5. For Augustine on demons, see *Teaching Christianity* 8, 14-15; 9, 2-3, 9:18-22.
6. *Revisions* I, 4, 1.
7. Reading *non possumus*.
8. On the actor Roscius, see Cicero, *De Oratore* 1, 130; and *Pro Quinto Roscio Comoedo*.
9. On the sculptor Myron, see Cicero, *Contra Verrem* 4, 135.
10. See *Order* II, 12, 37.
11. A less than convincing etymological derivation: *disciplina – discendo*.
12. On the punishments Augustine received as a schoolboy, and the terror they inspired, see *Confessions* I, 9, 14 and I, 14, 23.
13. Reading *partium*.
14. See Letter 3; *The Immortality of the Soul* 1, 5, 7, and 9.
15. The reference is most likely to Ambrose, whose eloquence Augustine praises in *Confessions* V, 1, 23. But Augustine at about this time also feels indebted to Theodorus (*The Happy Life* 1 and 4; but see *Revisions* 2).
16. The "other" is Zenobius; see *Order* 1, 20.
17. A fragment from the Roman tragic poet Pacuvius (ca. 220-130 B.C.E.), quoted by Cicero, *De inventione* 1, 27.
18. See *On Genesis: A Refutation of the Manicheans* I, 4, 7.
19. See *Order* II, 15, 43.
20. See *Revisions* I, 4, 4; *The Trinity* XII, 15, 24.
21. That is, in *The Immortality of the Soul*.

Index

In the Same Series from New City Press

The Augustine Catechism
The Enchiridion on Faith, Hope and Love
John E. Rotelle, O.S.A. (ed.)

"This is a recent translation by Bruce Harbert of St. Augustine's masterly, brief presentation of the Faith . . . which can speak as clearly to the faithful now as it did in the fifth century."
New Oxford Review

ISBN 1-56548-124-0, 3d printing, paper, 5 3/8 x 8 1/2, 144 pp.